India:
A Mosaic

- - - - -

India:
A Mosaic

- - - - -

By

Ian Buruma

Christopher de Bellaigue

Amartya Sen

Anita Desai

Roderick MacFarquhar

Hilary Mantel

Pankaj Mishra

Preface by

N. RAM

Introduction by

ARUNDHATI ROY

Edited by

ROBERT B. SILVERS AND
BARBARA EPSTEIN

NEW YORK REVIEW BOOKS

New York

THIS IS A NEW YORK REVIEW BOOK

PUBLISHED BY THE NEW YORK REVIEW OF BOOKS

INDIA: A MOSAIC

Published in 2000 in the United States of America by

The New York Review of Books

1755 Broadway

New York, NY 10019

Library of Congress Cataloging-in-Publication Data

India: a mosaic / Ian Buruma ... [et al.]; edited by Robert B. Silvers and
Barbara Epstein; with an introduction by Arundhati Roy.
   p.   cm.
   ISBN 0-940322-08-0 (hardcover: alk. paper)
   1. India. I. Buruma, Ian. II. Silvers, Robert B. III. Epstein,
Barbara, date.
DS407.I51325   2000
954—dc 21   99-32297
                                        CIP37

ISBN 0-940322-08-0

Printed in the United States of America on acid-free paper.

January 2000

www.nybooks.com

Contents

- - - - -

Acknowledgments

- - - - -

The editors would like to thank N. Ram, the editor of India's *Frontline* magazine, for his help and sound advice as well as for his hospitality in Chennai. We would also like to thank Leon Klayman for his selection and production of the enclosed CD demonstrating the wide and seductive range of Indian music.

Among the members of the staff of *The New York Review of Books* whom we particularly would like to thank are Borden Elniff, Diane Seltzer, Michael Shae, and Catherine Tice.

Preface

- - - - -

This is a book of essays selected from *The New York Review of Books* on contrasting facets of what may be called (changing merely the tense in the title of a book on India's ancient civilization by a well-known British historian, A. L. Basham) *The Wonder That Is India*. India is the land of diversities par excellence, "unity in diversity" (the Nehruvian, freedom-movement term of art), opposites, continuities, harmonies, inconsistencies, contradictions. It is multiethnic, multilingual, multireligious, multicultural, multipolitical. It is a confluence of streams of humanity in a sense and on a scale that are matched by few nation-states of the contemporary world. It has been described as a rich country with poor people. Its contemporary experience as a democracy is a combination of light and shade, the inspiring and the dispiriting, the upbeat and the downbeat, in a truly challenging and wondrous sense. Each of the writers presented in this book brings to his or her facet of India a distinctive standpoint, insight, or gaze.

Arundhati Roy, the world-renowned author of *The God of Small Things*, was invited to do an introduction to this group of essays on India. Meanwhile, on May 11 and 13, 1998, the Bharatiya Janata Party–led coalition government had stunned the world by conducting five underground nuclear explosions at Pokhran in the Rajasthan desert and declaring India the world's sixth nuclear-weapon state. Toward the end of that month, the inevitable answer came from Pakistan's Muslim League government: six nuclear explosions in the Chagai hills. Suddenly, South Asia appeared to be one of the world's most dangerous places. Pundits everywhere spoke of the initiation of a perilous new arms race between the two old rivals, the world's newest overt nuclear-weapon states.

Ms. Roy's response to this unimagined situation was an eight-thousand-word essay, "The End of Imagination," which appeared first in Indian publications and then found its way, in the English original as well as in translations, around the world. Passionately argued, unliteralist, antichauvinist, uncompromising, brilliantly written, it proved an influential intervention in the national and international debate on the Indian nuclear adventure. As the initial euphoria over the Pokhran explosions dissipated, as the political forces of the Hindu right suffered one setback after another, as "nuclear adventurism" seemed to swing toward (what opposition parties in the Indian parliament and critical voices in the Indian media have characterized as) "capitulation" to the discriminatory global nuclear order (spearheaded by the United States), the vital question that confronted the people of India as well as Pakistan was: How to get off the Tiger?

The opening of a new round of official Indo-Pakistani

contacts and dialogue—the cricket and transborder bus diplomacy (the former genuinely popular, the latter involving basically the spectacle of prime ministers playing ordinary bus-riding citizens by traveling modest distances across borders); the Lahore Declaration; and some promising nongovernmental, people-to-people interactions—all seem, in one way or another, to be a response to this somewhat desperate question. Both the Indian government's offer of "no first use of nuclear weapons" and "no use of nuclear weapons against any non–nuclear-weapon country" and the Pakistani government's intimation of a willingness to enter into an agreement with India on the nondeployment of nuclear weapons have been interpreted in some quarters as offering elements of hope. But the claims of de facto nuclear weaponization and minimum credible nuclear deterrent represent the other pole to what India's vigorous democratic campaign against nuclear weapons demands: no introduction and deployment of nuclear weapons; no conversion of fissile material stocks into nuclear weapons; no further nuclear testing; and de-weaponization (that is, dismantling the nuclear weapons in the small South Asian armories).

Ms. Roy's introduction, based on her longer essay and emphasizing some of its core propositions (including her distinctive ideas about the Idea of India and her plea for the rejection of antihumanistic jingoism and chauvinism) in a challenging, provocative way, sets the tone and mood for these essays, which offer their own distinctive voices and signatures.

N. RAM

Arundhati
Roy

- - - - -

INTRODUCTION

"THE DESERT SHOOK," the Government of India informed us (its people).

"The whole mountain turned white," the Government of Pakistan replied.

> By afternoon the wind had fallen silent over Pokhran. At 3:45 PM, the timer detonated the three devices. Around 200 to 300 m deep in the earth, the heat generated was equivalent to a million degrees centigrade—as hot as temperatures on the sun. Instantly, rocks weighing around a thousand tons, a mini mountain underground, vapourized.... Shockwaves from the blast began to lift a mound of earth the size of a football field by several metres. One scientist on seeing it said, "I can now believe stories of Lord Krishna lifting a hill."[1]

"These are not just nuclear tests, they are nationalism tests," we were repeatedly told.

---

1. *India Today*, May 1998.

This has been hammered home, over and over again. The bomb is India. India is the bomb. Not just India, Hindu India. Therefore, be warned, any criticism of it is not just antinational, but anti-Hindu. (Of course, in Pakistan the bomb is Islamic. Other than that, politically, the same physics applies.) This is one of the unexpected perks of having a nuclear bomb. Not only can the Government use it to threaten the Enemy, they can use it to declare war on their own people. Us.

In 1975, one year after India first dipped her toe into the nuclear sea, Mrs. Gandhi declared the Emergency. What will 1999 bring? There's talk of cells being set up to monitor antinational activity. Talk of amending cable laws to ban networks "harming national culture" (*The Indian Express*, July 3, 1998). Of churches being struck off the list of religious places because "wine is served" (announced in *The Indian Express* on July 3, 1998, and retracted in *The Times of India* on July 4, 1998). Artists, writers, actors, and singers are being harassed, threatened (and succumbing to the threats). Not just by goon squads but by instruments of the government. And in courts of law. There are letters and articles circulating on the Net—creative interpretations of Nostradamus's predictions claiming that a mighty, all-conquering Hindu nation is about to emerge, a resurgent India that will "burst forth upon its former oppressors and destroy them completely." That "the beginning of the terrible revenge [that will wipe out all Muslims] will be in the seventh month of 1999." This may well be the work of some lone nut, or a bunch of arcane god-squadders. The trouble is that having a nuclear bomb makes thoughts like these seem feasible. It creates thoughts like these. It bestows on people these utterly misplaced, utterly deadly notions of their own power. It's happening. It's all happening. I wish I could say "slowly but surely"—but I can't. Things are moving at a pretty fair clip.

When I told my friends that I was writing this piece, they cautioned me. "Go ahead," they said, "but first make sure you're not vulnerable. Make sure your papers are in order. Make sure your taxes are paid."

My papers are in order. My taxes are paid. But how can one not be vulnerable in a climate like this? Everyone is vulnerable. Accidents happen. There's safety only in acquiescence. As I write, I am filled with foreboding. In this country, I have truly known what it means for a writer to feel loved (and, to some degree, hated too). Last year I was one of the items being paraded in the media's end-of-the-year National Pride Parade. Among the others, much to my mortification, were a bomb maker and an international beauty queen. Each time a beaming person stopped me on the street and said "You have made India proud" (referring to the prize I won, not the book I wrote), I felt a little uneasy. It frightened me then and it terrifies me now, because I know how easily that swell, that tide of emotion, can turn against me. Perhaps the time for that has come. I'm going to step out from under the fairy lights and say what's on my mind.

It's this:

If protesting against having a nuclear bomb implanted in my brain is anti-Hindu and antinational, then I secede. I hereby declare myself an independent, mobile republic. I am a citizen of the earth. I own no territory. I have no flag. I'm female, but have nothing against eunuchs. My policies are simple. I'm willing to sign any nuclear nonproliferation treaty or nuclear test ban treaty that's going. Immigrants are welcome. You can help me design our flag.

My world has died. And I write to mourn its passing.

Admittedly it was a flawed world. An unviable world. A scarred and wounded world. It was a world that I myself have criticized unsparingly, but only because I loved it. It didn't deserve to die. It didn't deserve to be dismembered. Forgive me, I realize that sentimentality is uncool—but what shall I do with my desolation?

I loved it simply because it offered humanity a choice. It was a rock out at sea. It was a stubborn chink of light that insisted that there was a different way of living. It was a functioning possibility. A real option. All that's gone now. India's nuclear tests, the manner in which they were conducted, the euphoria with which they have been greeted (by us) is indefensible. To me, it signifies dreadful things. The end of imagination. The end of freedom actually, because, after all, that's what freedom is. Choice.

On the fifteenth of August last year we celebrated the fiftieth anniversary of India's independence. Next May we can mark our first anniversary in nuclear bondage.

Why did they do it?

Political expediency is the obvious, cynical answer, except that it only raises another, more basic question: Why should it have been politically expedient?

The three Official Reasons given are: China, Pakistan, and Exposing Western Hypocrisy.

Taken at face value, and examined individually, they're somewhat baffling. I'm not for a moment suggesting that these are not real issues. Merely that they aren't new. The only new thing on the old horizon is the Indian Government. In his appallingly cavalier letter to the US President (why bother to write at all if you're going to write like this?) our Prime Minister says India's decision to go ahead with the nuclear tests was due to a "deteriorating security environment." He goes on to mention the war with China in 1962 and the "three aggressions we have suffered in the last fifty years [from Pakistan]. And for the last ten years we have been the victim of unremitting terrorism and militancy sponsored by it . . . especially in Jammu and Kashmir."

The war with China is thirty-five years old. Unless there's some vital state secret that we don't know about, it certainly seemed as though matters had improved slightly between us. Just a few days before the nuclear tests General Fu Quanyou, Chief of General Staff of the Chinese People's Liberation Army, was the guest of our Chief of Army Staff. We heard no words of war.

The most recent war with Pakistan was fought twenty-seven years ago. Admittedly Kashmir continues to be a deeply troubled region and no doubt Pakistan is gleefully fanning the flames. But surely there must be flames to fan in the first place? Surely the kindling is crackling and ready to burn? Can the Indian State with even a modicum of honesty absolve itself completely of having a hand in Kashmir's troubles? Kashmir, and for that matter, Assam, Tripura, Nagaland—virtually the whole of the Northeast—Jharkhand, Uttarakhand, and all the trouble that's still to come, these are symptoms of a deeper malaise. It cannot and will not be solved by pointing nuclear missiles at Pakistan.

Even Pakistan can't be solved by pointing nuclear missiles at Pakistan. Though we are separate countries, we share skies, we share winds, we share water. Where radioactive fallout will land on any given day depends on the direction of the wind and rain. Lahore and Amritsar are thirty miles apart. If we bomb Lahore, Punjab will burn. If we bomb Karachi, then Gujarat and Rajasthan—perhaps even Bombay—will burn. Any nuclear war with Pakistan will be a war against ourselves.

As for the third Official Reason: Exposing Western Hypocrisy—how much more exposed can it be? Which decent human being on earth harbors any illusions about it? These are people whose histories are spongy with the blood of others. Colonialism, apartheid, slavery, ethnic cleansing, germ warfare, chemical weapons—they virtually invented it all. They have plundered nations, snuffed out civilizations, exterminated entire populations. They stand on the world's stage stark naked but entirely unembarrassed, because they know that they have more money, more food, and bigger bombs than anybody else. They know they can wipe us out in the course of an ordinary working day. Personally, I'd say it is more arrogance than hypocrisy.

We have less money, less food, and smaller bombs.

However, we have, or had, all kinds of other wealth. Delightful, unquantifiable. What we've done with it is the opposite of what we think we've done. We've pawned it all. We've traded it in. For what? In order to enter into a contract with the very people we claim to despise. In the larger scheme of things, we've agreed to play their game and play it their way. We've accepted their terms and conditions unquestioningly. The Comprehensive Test Ban Treaty ain't nothin' com pared to this.

All in all, I think it is fair to say that we're the hypocrites. We're the ones who've abandoned what was arguably a moral position: i.e., we have the technology, we can make bombs if we want to, but we won't. We don't believe in them.

We're the ones who have now set up this craven clamoring to be admitted into the club of Superpowers. (If we are, we will no doubt gladly slam the door after us, and say to hell with principles about fighting Discriminatory World Orders.) For India to demand the status of a Superpower is as ridiculous as demanding to play in the World Cup finals simply because we have a ball. Never mind that we haven't qualified, or that we don't play much soccer and haven't got a team.

Since we've chosen to enter the arena, it might be an idea to begin by learning the rules of the game. Rule number one is Acknowledge the Masters. Who are the best players? The ones with more money, more food, more bombs.

Rule number two is Locate Yourself in Relation to

Them: i.e., make an honest assessment of your position and abilities. The honest assessment of ourselves (in quantifiable terms) reads as follows:

We are a nation of nearly a billion people. In development terms we rank number 138 out of the 175 countries listed in the UNDP's Human Development Index. More than four hundred million of our people are illiterate and live in absolute poverty, over six hundred million lack even basic sanitation, and over two hundred million have no safe drinking water.

So the three Official Reasons, taken individually, don't hold much water. However, if you link them, a kind of twisted logic reveals itself. It has more to do with us than them.

The key words in our Prime Minister's letter to the US President were "suffered" and "victim." That's the substance of it. That's our meat and drink. We need to feel like victims. We need to feel beleaguered. We need enemies. We have so little sense of ourselves as a nation and therefore constantly cast about for targets to define ourselves against. Prevalent political wisdom suggests that to prevent the State from crumbling, we need a national cause, and other than our currency (and, of course, poverty, illiteracy, and elections), we have none. This is the heart of the matter. This is the road that has led us to the bomb. This search for selfhood. If we are looking for a way out, we need some honest answers to some uncomfortable questions. Once again, it isn't as though these questions haven't been asked before. It's just that we prefer to mumble the answers and hope that no one's heard.

Is there such a thing as an Indian identity?

Do we really need one?

Who is an Authentic Indian and who isn't?

Is India Indian?

Does it matter?

Whether or not there has ever been a single civilization that could call itself "Indian Civilization," whether or not India was, is, or ever will become a cohesive cultural entity, depends on whether you dwell on the differences or the similarities in the cultures of the people who have inhabited the subcontinent for centuries. India, as a modern nation-state, was marked out with precise geographical boundaries, in their precise geographical way, by a British Act of Parliament in 1899. Our country, as we know it, was forged on the anvil of the British Empire for the entirely unsentimental reasons of commerce and administration. But even as she was born, she began her struggle against her creators. So is India Indian? It's a tough question. Let's just say that we're an ancient people learning to live in a recent nation.

What is true is that India is an artificial State—a State that was created by a government, not a people. A State created from the top down, not the bottom up. The majority of India's citizens will not (to this day) be able to identify her boundaries on a map, or say which language is spoken where or which god is worshiped in what region. Most are too poor and too uneducated to have even an elementary idea of the extent and complexity of their own country. The impoverished, illiterate agrarian majority have no stake in the State.

And indeed, why should they, how can they, when they don't even know what the State is? To them, India is, at best, a noisy slogan that comes around during the elections. Or a montage of people on Government TV programs wearing regional costumes and saying "Mera Bharat Mahan."

The people who have a vital stake (or, more to the point, a business interest) in India having a single, lucid, cohesive national identity are the politicians who constitute our national political parties. The reason isn't far to seek: it's simply because their struggle, their career goal, is—and must necessarily be—to become that identity. To be identified with that identity. If there isn't one, they have to manufacture one and persuade people to vote for it. It isn't their fault. It comes with the territory. It is inherent in the nature of our system of centralized government. A congenital defect in our particular brand of democracy. The greater the numbers of illiterate people, the poorer the country, and the more morally bankrupt the politicians, the cruder the ideas of what that identity should be. In a situation like this, illiteracy is not just sad, it's downright dangerous. However, to be fair, cobbling together a viable predigested "National Identity" for India would be a formidable challenge even for the wise and the visionary. Every single Indian citizen could, if he or she wants to, claim to belong to some minority or another. The fissures, if you look for them, run vertically, horizontally, layered, whorled, circular, spiral, inside out, and outside in. Fires, when they're lit, race along any one of these schisms, and in the process release tremendous

bursts of political energy. Not unlike what happens
when you split an atom.

It is this energy that Gandhi sought to harness when
he rubbed the magic lamp and invited Ram and Rahim
to partake of human politics and India's war of independence against the British. It was a sophisticated,
magnificent, imaginative struggle, but its objective was
simple and lucid, the target highly visible, easy to identify, and succulent with political sin. In the circumstances, the energy found an easy focus. The trouble is
that the circumstances are entirely changed now, but
the genie is out of its lamp and won't go back in. (It
could be sent back, but nobody wants it to go, it's
proved itself too useful.) Yes, it won us freedom. But it
also won us the carnage of Partition. And now, in the
hands of lesser statesmen, it has won us the Hindu
Nuclear Bomb.

To be fair to Gandhi and to other leaders of the
National Movement, they did not have the benefit of
hindsight and could not possibly have known what the
eventual, long-term consequences of their strategy
would be. They could not have predicted how quickly
the situation would careen out of control. They could
not have foreseen what would happen when they
passed their flaming torches into the hands of their successors, or how venal those hands could be.

It was Indira Gandhi who started the real slide. It
is she who made the genie a permanent State Guest.
She injected the venom into our political veins. She
invented our particularly vile local brand of political
expediency. She showed us how to conjure enemies out

of thin air, how to fire at phantoms that she had carefully fashioned for that very purpose. It was she who discovered the benefits of never burying the dead, but preserving their putrid carcasses and trundling them out to worry old wounds when it suited her. Between herself and her sons she managed to bring the country to its knees. Our new Government has just kicked us over and arranged our heads on the chopping block.

The Bharatiya Janata Party (BJP) is, in some senses, a specter that Indira Gandhi and the Congress created. Or, if you want to be less harsh, a specter that fed and reared itself in the political spaces and communal suspicion that the Congress nourished and cultivated. It has put a new complexion on the politics of governance. While Mrs. Gandhi played hidden games with politicians and their parties, she reserved a shrill convent-school rhetoric, replete with tired platitudes, to address the general public. The BJP, on the other hand, has chosen to light its fires directly on the streets and in the homes and hearts of people. It is prepared to do by day what the Congress would do only by night. To legitimize what was previously considered unacceptable (but done anyway). There is perhaps a fragile case to be made here in favor of hypocrisy. Could the hypocrisy of the Congress Party, the fact that they conduct their wretched affairs surreptitiously instead of openly, could that possibly mean there is a tiny glimmer of guilt somewhere? Some small fragment of remembered decency?

Actually, no.

No.

What am I doing? Why am I foraging for scraps of hope?

The way it has worked—in the case of the demolition of the Babri Masjid as well as in the making of the nuclear bomb—is that the Congress sowed the seeds, tended the crop, then the BJP stepped in and reaped the hideous harvest. They waltz together, locked in each others' arms. They're inseparable, despite their professed differences. Between them they have brought us here, to this dreadful, dreadful place.

The jeering, hooting young men who battered down the Babri Masjid are the same ones whose pictures appeared in the papers in the days that followed the nuclear tests. They were on the streets, celebrating India's nuclear bomb and simultaneously "condemning Western Culture" by emptying crates of Coke and Pepsi into public drains. I'm a little baffled by their logic: Coke is Western Culture, but the nuclear bomb is an old Indian tradition?

Yes, I've heard—the bomb is in the Vedas. It might be, but if you look hard enough, you'll find Coke in the Vedas, too. That's the great thing about all religious texts. You can find anything you want in them—as long as you know what you're looking for.

But returning to the subject of the non-Vedic 1990s: we storm the heart of whiteness, we embrace the most diabolical creation of Western science and call it our own. But we protest against their music, their food, their clothes, their cinema, and their literature. That's not hypocrisy. That's humor.

It's funny enough to make a skull smile.

We're back on the old ship. The S. S. *Authenticity &* *Indianness.*

If there is going to be a pro-authenticity/antinational drive, perhaps the government ought to get its history straight and its facts right. If they're going to do it, they may as well do it properly.

First of all, the original inhabitants of this land were not Hindu. Ancient though it is, there were human beings on earth before there was Hinduism. India's tribal people have a greater claim to being indigenous to this land than anybody else, and how are they treated by the State and its minions? Oppressed, cheated, robbed of their lands, shunted around like surplus goods. Perhaps a good place to start would be to restore to them the dignity that was once theirs. Perhaps the Government could make a public undertaking that more dams like the Sardar Sarovar on the Narmada will not be built, that more people will not be displaced.

But, of course, that would be inconceivable, wouldn't it? Why? Because it's impractical. Because tribal people don't really matter. Their histories, their customs, their deities are dispensable. They must learn to sacrifice these things for the greater good of the Nation (that has snatched from them everything they ever had).

Okay, so that's out.

For the rest, I could compile a practical list of things to ban and buildings to break. It'll need some research, but off the top of my head, here are a few suggestions.

They could begin by banning a number of ingredients from our cuisine: chilies (Mexico), tomatoes (Peru), potatoes (Bolivia), coffee (Morocco), tea, white sugar, cinnamon (China)—they could then move into recipes. Tea with milk and sugar, for instance (Britain). Smoking will be out of the question. Tobacco came from North America.

Cricket, English, and Democracy should be forbidden. Either kabaddi or kho-kho could replace cricket. I don't want to start a riot, so I hesitate to suggest a replacement for English. (Italian? It has found its way to us via a kinder route: marriage, not Imperialism.) We have already discussed (earlier in this essay) the emerging, apparently acceptable alternative to Democracy.

All hospitals in which Western medicine is practiced or prescribed should be shut down. All national newspapers discontinued. The railways dismantled. Airports closed. And what about our newest toy—the mobile phone? Can we live without it, or shall I suggest that they make an exception there? They could put it down in the column marked "Universal"? (Only essential commodities will be included here. No music, art, or literature.)

Needless to say, sending your children to university in the US and rushing there yourself to have your prostate operated upon will be a cognizable offense.

The building demolition drive could begin with the Rashtrapati Bhavan and gradually spread from cities to the countryside, culminating in the destruction of all monuments (mosques, churches, temples) that were built on what was once tribal or forest land.

It will be a long, long list. It would take years of work. I couldn't use a computer because that wouldn't be very authentic of me, would it?

I don't mean to be facetious, merely to point out that this is surely the shortcut to hell. There's no such thing as an Authentic India or a Real Indian. There is no Divine Committee that has the right to sanction one single, authorized version of what India is or should be. There is no one religion or language or caste or region or person or story or book that can claim to be its sole representative. There are, and can only be, visions of India, various ways of seeing it—honest, dishonest; wonderful, absurd; modern, traditional; male, female. They can be argued over, criticized, praised, scorned, but not banned or broken. Not hunted down.

Railing against the past will not heal us. History has happened. It's over and done with. All we can do is to change its course by encouraging what we love instead of destroying what we don't. There is beauty yet in this brutal, damaged world of ours. Hidden, fierce, immense. Beauty that is uniquely ours and beauty that we have received with grace from others, enhanced, re-invented, and made our own. We have to seek it out, nurture it, love it. Making bombs will only destroy us. It doesn't matter whether we use them or not. They will destroy us either way.

India's nuclear bomb is the final act of betrayal by a ruling class that has failed its people.

However many garlands we heap on our scientists, however many medals we pin to their chests, the truth is that it's far easier to make a bomb than to educate four hundred million people.

According to opinion polls, we're expected to believe that there's a national consensus on the issue. It's official now. Everybody loves the bomb. (Therefore, the bomb is good.)

Is it possible for a man who cannot write his own name to understand even the basic, elementary facts about the nature of nuclear weapons? Has anybody told him that nuclear war has nothing at all to do with his received notions of war? Nothing to do with honor, nothing to do with pride? Has anybody bothered to explain to him about thermal blasts, radioactive fallout, and the nuclear winter? Are there even words in his language to describe the concepts of enriched uranium, fissile material, and critical mass? Or has his language itself become obsolete? Is he trapped in a time capsule, watching the world pass him by, unable to understand or communicate with it because his language never took into account the horrors that the human race would dream up? Does he not matter at all, this man? Shall we just treat him like some kind of a cretin? If he asks any questions, ply him with iodine pills and parables about how Lord Krishna lifted a hill or how the destruction of Lanka by Hanuman was unavoidable in order to preserve Sita's virtue and Ram's reputation? Use his own beautiful stories as weapons against him? Shall we release him from his capsule only during elections, and once he's voted, shake him by the hand, flatter him with some bullshit about the Wisdom of the Common Man, and send him right back in?

I'm not talking about one man, of course; I'm talking about millions and millions of people who live in this country. This is their land too, you know. They have the right to make an informed decision about its fate and, as far as I can tell, nobody has informed them about anything. The tragedy is that nobody could, even if they wanted to. Truly, literally, there's no language to do it in. This is the real horror of India. The orbits of the powerful and the powerless spinning further and further apart from each other, never intersecting, sharing nothing. Not a language. Not even a country.

Who the hell conducted those opinion polls? Who the hell is the Prime Minister to decide whose finger will be on the nuclear button that could turn everything we love—our earth, our skies, our mountains, our plains, our rivers, our cities and villages—to ash in an instant? Who the hell is he to reassure us that there will be no accidents? How does he know? Why should we trust him? What has he ever done to make us trust him? What have any of them ever done to make us trust them?

The nuclear bomb is the most antidemocratic, antinational, antihuman, outright evil thing that man has ever made.

If you are religious, then remember that this bomb is Man's challenge to God.

It's worded quite simply: We have the power to destroy everything that You have created.

If you're not religious, then look at it this way. This world of ours is 4,600 million years old.

It could end in an afternoon.

JULY 15, 1998

India:
A Mosaic

- - - - -

Ian
Buruma

- - - - -

INDIA:

THE PERILS

OF

DEMOCRACY

Chandigarh is Great
Because it has a thought embedded
in its Foundations
To generate a System
To generate an Order
To show a Way
To enrich Life[1]

---

1. From Aditya Prakash, *Chandigarh: A Presentation in Free Verse,* published in Chandigarh by the author himself.

1

- - - - -

ONE OF THE oddest bits of information I picked
up in Chandigarh, the capital of Haryana and Punjab,
designed more or less from scratch by Le Corbusier in
the early 1950s, was that none of its trees is from India.
I was told that every tree in this modern garden city in
northwest India was transplanted from abroad. I don't
know whether this is strictly true; probably not, but
it is the sort of thing you would hear in Chandigarh.
Like the rather pleasant but wholly man-made Sukhna
Lake, it adds yet another touch of artificiality to a
completely invented town of geometrical roundabouts
and avenues with names like V-2 Vertical or V-4
Horizontal. "Chandigarh," exclaimed an Indian academic whom I visited in Delhi, "is a symbol of all that
is inauthentic about modern urban India."

It depends, of course, on what one means by inauthentic. The idea of Chandigarh, conceived by Jawaharlal Nehru, prime minister at the time of the city's
(and post-imperial India's) birth, was that it should be
a new town, "symbolic of the freedom of India, unfet-
tered by the traditions of the past . . . an expression of

the nation's faith in the future." The Indian past was stained by centuries of humiliation. The Moghul style of Muslim invaders certainly wouldn't do for a new Indian republic, nor would the Gothic or Indo-Saracenic fripperies of the British Raj. And since Nehru's vision was of a modern, secular, democratic, internationalist state, some revamped Hindu style was hardly fitting either. As Sunil Khilnani observes in *The Idea of India*[2], his splendid book about definitions of the Indian nation, Nehru wanted India "to move forward by one decisive act that broke both with its ancient and its more recent history." And so the city was built in the rationalist, International style, on an empty plain, after the removal of a few hundred villagers who would only budge once they had been reassured that they would be shot if they refused—thus government authority was proved to be genuine.

Le Corbusier had been waiting all his life for a leader like Nehru. He always had wanted to build a grand monument or, better still, an entire city for a brave new world: the Palace of the League of Nations in 1927, the Palace of Soviets in 1931, "Radiant Cities" for Mussolini and Marshal Pétain, the United Nations headquarters in 1947. But all these plans came to nothing. Now, at last, in 1950, when two representatives of the Punjab government, Chief Engineer P. L. Varna and Public Works Administrator P. N. Thapar, knocked on his door at 35, rue de Sèvres, in Paris, his chance had come. "Corbu" started on a typically imperious note. When

---

2. Farrar, Straus and Giroux, 1998.

invited to work in India, he told his guests that he could design their city just as well in Paris, and sent them off to Marseilles to admire his famous apartment building, Unité d'Habitation.

In the event, Corbu did go to India, twenty-two times. The basic plan for the city of Chandigarh was drawn up in a matter of hours. Corbu arrived, took out a sheet of paper and a crayon, and declared: "*Voici la tête,*" marking down the government buildings, "*et voilà l'estomac, le cité-centre.*" He knew his mind. "Doctrine," he liked to say, "triumphs, and leads us along." That is to say, Corbu's doctrine. He enjoyed working in India. He found the workers, including women beavering away in colorful saris, "picturesque." They were also very cheap. Workers were paid a pittance and were not even housed. But as Corbu remarked, "the advantage of slavery in *high* and noble works of architecture"[3] was that one could change one's mind on the spot, without worrying about escalating costs.

Corbu, then, was, as Khilnani dryly states, "an odd choice as democratic India's first architect." Yet he and Nehru seem to have understood each other, and played parallel roles. Khilnani, a political scientist who is currently working on Nehru's biography, argues that constitutional democracy, based on universal suffrage, was handed down to his people by Nehru, not because of any great popular demand for it, but because Nehru believed in it. Having set up the institutions of

---

3. *Le Corbusier: Architect of the Century* (London: Arts Council of Great Britain, 1987), p. 283.

democracy, Nehru would act as a kind of benevolent guide in secular politics: through practice, Indians would gradually get used to the mechanics of democracy. The tools—and buildings—came first, the rest would follow. The core of Khilnani's argument is that Nehru's political idea of India, focused on the state, was the one thing all Indians, whatever their caste or creed, would have in common. "The state," in Khilnani's words, "etched itself into the imagination of Indians in a way that no previous political agency had ever done."

Just so, Corbu saw himself as a "friendly shepherd," a *berger amical*, for aspiring Indian architects. Peter the Great brought European architects to St. Petersburg to show Russians how to build a civilized city, and in the process import modern European civilization itself. Chandigarh was Nehru's Petersburg, and Corbu was his civilizer. It was as though the buildings would forge a new attitude to politics, to culture, to life.

One of the criticisms most often made of both Nehru and Corbu was their disregard for Indian conditions and traditions. If only Nehru's idea of India had "reflected" the religious and cultural feelings of ordinary Indians more, so I was told by several intelligent people in India, the current backlash of Hindu chauvinism might never have come.

But it is unclear just how such feelings ought to have been reflected in government. Even the Hindu chauvinists are confused and divided over this. Some simply want to bash Muslims, while others want to turn India into a Hindu state. But since Hindus are a highly diverse people, with many different sects, and Hinduism never was a unified religion in the way of Islam or Christianity, the idea of a Hindu state has to be vague at best. Gandhi's vision of India as a spiritual village society still has its admirers, but it is hardly practical.

9

Khilnani's book is a masterful rebuttal to all cultural romantics and religious chauvinists. I think he is right when he says that Nehru "fully recognized the depth and plurality of religious beliefs in India. It was precisely this that convinced him of the need to keep social identities outside the political arena." Again the parallel with Corbu's modernist internationalism is striking. As Khilnani puts it, in a passage on Chandigarh: "In celebrating a wholly alien form, style and material, it aspired to a neutrality, a zero-degree condition that would make it equally resistant to the claims upon it of any and all cultural or religious groups." But Nehru—Harrow, Cambridge, and Fabian socialism notwithstanding—was also an Indian nationalist. He did not simply want to copy the West. And Corbu's Chandigarh was not meant to look like Europe. In a letter to his collaborators, Corbu said he strove after an "organic architecture . . . which is neither English, nor French, nor American, but Indian of the second half of the 20th century."[4]

Curiously, Corbu liked to use the word "Hindu" instead of "Indian." Three "Hindu architects" were to be attached to his Paris office, to receive an education in modernism, which remained in touch with "the Hindu civilization." Corbu never made it clear what he meant

---

4. Letter from Le Corbusier, December 12, 1951.

by Hindu civilization. How could he? But perhaps his use of the term was Nehruvian too, in the sense that Nehru himself, while fighting all his life against caste prejudice, led a government that was dominated by high-caste Hindus. And Chandigarh, the home of bureaucrats, is nothing if not a high-caste Hindu city.

How has it all held up? I arrived in Chandigarh by train from Delhi. Indian trains have a class system, which is almost as complex as the order of castes. There are six classes. I was sitting in "A/C chair car," which ranks above "ordinary first class," but below "A/C first class," I think. Next to me was a well-dressed young Punjabi, full of bouncing energy, who worked for a paint company. He loved Chandigarh. In words I was to hear again, it was "neat and clean," so unlike Delhi, "a terrible place." With one police-man for every hundred citizens, Chandigarh is also a very secure city. My companion loved Chandigarh precisely because it was not like the rest of India. But, he admitted, "the showing-off element is also there: big houses, Mercedes-Benz, even Pierre Cardin, they are there."

Chandigarh was built as a city of government. There is no industry to speak of, and not all that much com-merce either. The first thing you notice on arrival at the station, apart from its remarkable cleanliness, is bureaucratic procedure. Instead of the free-for-all scramble that takes place elsewhere, you have to stand in line for a prepaid ticket for motor-rickshaws and taxis, with the result that everyone waits around end-lessly: neat and clean, disciplined even, but hopelessly inefficient. As is true of other modern garden cities, such as Canberra, it is hard to tell where the city begins, or even if there is a city at all. You see straight roads and roundabouts, with bungalows and modern buildings peeping through the shrubbery. The "center," called Sector 17, consists of a baking hot concrete square surrounded by shops. No one lives there. After 7:30 it is dead. Everyone will have gone home, to Sector 9, or 16, or 25, depending on one's rank in the bureaucratic hierarchy. The lower the number, the higher your rank. Corbu's showcase government buildings, the Secretariat, the High Court, and the Legislative Assembly, are in Sector 1.

But you don't see Sector 1 until you are right in it. For between the "temples of democracy" (Nehru's phrase) and the rest of the city is a vast space of trees, scrubland, and parks, filled, presumably, with those imported trees. The government buildings, huge in scale, yet oddly humbled by the view of the Himalayas on the horizon, have grandeur and beauty. To say they are too grand for a provincial government is to miss the point: these temples were meant to represent so much more than Haryana and Punjab.

Concrete looks better against the pale blue sky of northern India than in the watery gloom of western Europe. And Corbu's sculptural genius is clear to see: in the curved roof of the Assembly, or the sun-breaking overhang on the façade of the High Court, with its astonishing splashes of green, red, and yellow. There are few decorations, of course, since Corbu's modernism forbade that. But what decoration there is reflects not modern India, or "Hindu civilization," but Corbu's own mystical doodles: open hands, symbols of sun worship, and the male figure, representing Corbu's ideal proportions, known as the Modulor.[5]

It is tempting to read metaphors into Corbu's urban monuments stuck out there in the Punjabi plain. Each to his own preoccupations: Nirad Chaudhuri, the Bengali prophet of decadence, once compared Chandigarh to the Rolls Royces acquired and then abandoned by desert maharajas.[6] In his view, all forms of superior foreign civilization go to seed in the tropical sun. Others, younger and more to the left of the political spectrum, see Chandigarh as a mark of Indian subservience to Western models and masters. Yogendra Yadav, a political scientist in Delhi who complained to me about Chandigarh's inauthenticity, was one of them. He told me that Corbusier "doesn't exist in India, or in France, but inside ourselves." This doesn't mean that Indians of Nehru's generation weren't nationalists. They were, and often anti-Western too. (Interestingly, Corbu saw France and India as natural allies against "Americanism.") But India, like most developing nations, has been prone to mimic those whose power it fears.

A young teacher at the College of Architecture told me how Corbu had become an Indian guru. "We follow his rules blindly," the professor said. "That is our

5. The most detailed description of Le Corbusier's Chandigarh and its history is in Norma Evenson, *Chandigarh* (University of California Press, 1966).

6. *Hindustan Times Weekly,* 1969.

tradition." Nothing in the main government buildings can be changed. And there it all is to this day, a little torn at the edges, but maintained with the same loving care Indians lavish on their Ambassador cars, modeled on the 1956 Morris Oxford. And one can see, scattered across India, gimcrack versions of Corbu's designs: schools, banks, museums, apartment blocks, and so on. Some of them have remained empty. A museum curator in Delhi explained this to me with a shrug that expressed years of frustration: "In India, once a building goes up, it is recorded as being finished, without thinking about what to do with it."

Khilnani regards Chandigarh as a failure. It never produced "a society of secular individuals or a modernist politics. . . ." You see what he means right there in Sector 1. The Assembly, half of which is given to the legislature of Punjab and half to that of Haryana, is surrounded by steel fences and barbed wire, guarded by policemen with machine guns. You need a special permit to even get close to the temples of democracy. The reason for all this security is the car-bomb killing of Punjab's chief minister by Sikh separatists two years ago. I was shown around by Sumit Kumar, secretary of the Secretariat. We stood in front of the Assembly and gazed across an immense plaza, a kind of concrete lake, on the other side of which you could make out the stark outlines of the High Court. Corbu designed the plaza as a meeting place for Chandigarh's democratic citizens, who would gather there to discuss the politics of the day, like modern Athenians. It was deserted. Weeds sprouted here and there. "Security problems,"

said Mr. Kumar. Did people come here before the terrorist attack? "Not really," he said.

On one level, then, Chandigarh is the hollow shell
of Indian democracy, a representation without content, a museum to the deadly rationalism of a French
modernist architect and the naive optimism of the first
Indian prime minister after Independence. Until this
year, the citizens of Chandigarh didn't even vote for
their own local government. Chandigarh was governed
directly from New Delhi. At best, this Indian Brasília is
a comfortable suburb for administrators and retired
army officers, who dislike the squalid hurly-burly of
urban India.

But there is, in fact, a little more to it. For once you
get beyond first impressions, you notice how improvisation has humanized, and indeed "Indianized," some
of Corbu's rationalism. Corbu designed huge car parks,
at a time when the main form of transportation was
the bullock cart. And wide shopping streets were
built, instead of the customary open-air markets. Soon
many of the car parks were turned into bazaars, not by
architects but by ordinary citizens. "Non-planned
development" is the phrase. The best examples of non-
planned development are the slums, on the edges of
town. There you can see not only the invasion of
Corbu's urban dream by poor, village India, but also
signs that Nehru's political ideals have actually worked
after a fashion.

The slums are not called slums, but "colonies." Poor
workers were never supposed to stay in Chandigarh.
After building Corbu's monuments, they were meant to

disappear to wherever they had come from. In fact, of course, they stayed, in illegal settlements which are really displaced villages. At first, the government would send in armed policemen to chase the people away and burn down their dwellings. But in time, as Nehru's democracy took root, politicians began to see profit in the situation. In return for votes from the poor, they promised to legalize this colony and that. There were even cases where opposition politicians had slums set on fire, so they could promise to build them up again, if they got elected. In this rough-and-ready way, state patronage is beginning to seep down to the lowest castes, through their elected representatives.

You can tell a northern Indian slum by the presence of pigs rooting in the filth of the surrounding area, where men and boys squat in the grass to relieve themselves. I picked my way into a colony near the university, in the company of Mr. Kumar, looking immaculate in a cream suit, and a lawyer from the High Court, who held a white handkerchief to his nose. As slums in India go, this one was not so bad. Houses were made of mud and bricks. Some had roofs of corrugated iron. Many were covered in blue plastic sheets. Electricity was tapped from the wires passing overhead—illegally of course, but tolerated because of political protection. There were even TV sets. ("Television they want," said Mr. Kumar, "but not schools.") There was no sense of menace. People looked at us without interest. They were poorly dressed, the children often in rags. Many would have been Dalits, the lowest caste, whose traditional occupations, rag-picking, latrine-cleaning, sweeping, corpse-burying, and leather-curing, used to make them "untouchable." The others would have been from "other backward classes," or OBCs, who tend to be better off.

"These people," explained Mr. Kumar, "have the power now. The politicians don't care two hoots about us." Here he pointed at his cream-suited chest. "But these people are the majority in India, and they all vote." He did not say this in anger. But he was worried. For, as he put it, "good men don't get elected." Unscrupulous low-caste demagogues, who make irresponsible promises to the poor, are now voted in. For good government, he went on, you need good people. But there were too many ill-educated scoundrels in Indian politics now. "When you appeal to your caste, you go up, and when you are rational, you are going down. That is the nature of our politics now."

So Khilnani is probably right. The idea of the state as a patron has taken hold of the Indian imagination, though perhaps not quite in the way Nehru had intended. In the last ten years or so, politics has divided Indians more than ever along caste and regional lines. Nehru's idea of India has disintegrated into ideas of being a Hindu, a Tamil, or a Dalit. But Khilnani makes another case, which demands a degree of liberal optimism. He says that "constitutional democracy has proved to be the most reliable instrument available" for "civilizing political power." I like to believe that this is true. But India has a way of stretching one's faith to the limit.

2

- - - - -

THE DEATH OF Nehruvian secularism is sometimes given a precise date: December 6, 1992. Communal poison had been dripping into Indian politics before, but on that day a mob of Hindu fanatics tore down an unused sixteenth-century mosque in Ayodhya, called the Babri Masjid, because they believed that it had been constructed by Babur, founder of the Moghul dynasty, on the birth site of Ram, the mythical Hindu king. According to legend, there once had been a Ram temple there, and Hindu chauvinists vowed to "restore" it.

They came pouring into Ayodhya from other parts of Uttar Pradesh, as well as from Gujarat and Maharashtra in the west, Andra Pradesh in the center, and even Karnataka in the south—wild-haired, half-naked sadhus (Hindu ascetics), militant activists, urban youths in jeans and yellow headbands, true believers, and riffraff out for some violent sport. Most Muslims had fled, scared out of their wits by cars speeding through their neighborhoods, playing prerecorded sounds of riots and screams. For several years, the Hindu nationalists had been driven into a frenzy by politicians baying for Muslim blood on videos and cassette tapes, by TV soap operas about Ram and other Hindu heroes, and by stories in the press of Hindu "martyrdom," after an earlier attempt to storm the mosque had ended in violence.

To egg them on further, there was the pseudo-religious procession of L. K. Advani, a former movie journalist and current leader of the Hindu nationalist Bharatiya Janata Party (BJP), who was driven, like a god-king, from Gujarat to Ayodhya in a Toyota dressed up as a chariot in a Hindu epic. The stated aim of the Hindu nationalists' campaign was to build a new Ram temple on the site of the mosque. The real purpose was to mobilize a nationwide community of Hindus to vote for the BJP. The main challenge to Nehru's vision came not from the hysterical mob but from politicians who had taken communalism into the mainstream of Indian politics.

By the time the rioters were dispersed on December 7, thirteen Muslim men and children, who had been unable to get away, had been murdered with knives and pickaxes. (Many more died in riots that erupted elsewhere.) More than twenty mosques were damaged. Muslim houses and shops were looted and burned to the ground. And the police, mostly low-caste Hindus, encouraged the mob by giggling at the violence or looking the other way. The looters sang a song in praise of Durga, the mother goddess. It went:

> *Mother, your sons are calling you.*
> *Come down; we shall cut our heads off and offer*
>   *them to you.*
> *Bring your drinking bowl and we will fill it*
>   *with blood.*
> *Listen to my pleas,*
> *Fulfil my wishes,*

Give me Ayodhya,
give me Mathura, give me Kashi.[7]

Mathura is said to be the birthplace of Krishna, the divine hero who married 16,000 milkmaids and fathered 160,000 children, and Kashi is the holy city of Benares, where another mosque was built by the Moghuls on the site of a Hindu temple. Both are yet to be "liberated" by the Hindu mobs. The Benares mosque is closely guarded by armed police behind high fences.

Ayodhya is a complete contrast to Chandigarh: four hundred miles to the southeast of Corbu's city, it is ancient, it is dirty, and it is full of temples, some of them very dilapidated, painted powder-blue, egg-yellow, or pistachio-green. It is located in the middle of Uttar Pradesh, the state in the Hindi belt which produced not just Nehru himself but eight of thirteen Indian prime ministers since Independence. Muslims make up about 10 percent of the Ayodhya population, and until recent events they have lived there in peace. The clothes of Hindu priests are made largely by Muslim tailors. By the time I visited Ayodhya in October, most of the Muslims had come home. Local people didn't want trouble, I was told. It had all been the work of "outsiders."

I was taken to a temple, managed by a bankrupt businessman from Bihar. In the courtyard was a group of widows, old and young, who chanted praises to

---

7. Quoted from an excellent book on the riots by Ashis Nandy, Shika Trivedy, Shaul Mayaram, and Achyut Yagnik, *Creating a Nationality* (Delhi: Oxford University Press, 1995).

Ram. They were literally singing for their supper, for without the right to inherit, they were a burden on their families. I had been told that a powerful figure in the Vishva Hindu Parishad, or VHP, was staying at the temple. Since the VHP, a militant organization founded in 1964 to forge a unified Hindu community, had played a vital part in the Ayodhya affair, and was in effect the radical wing of the BJP, I was interested in meeting him. His name was Acharya Giriraj Kishore, the secretary general. After being thoroughly frisked by a bodyguard, I was shown into his presence.

Kishore was a small, round man, with long white hair. He lay on his bed, his pudgy hands glittering with gold. White caste marks were daubed on his forehead. The bodyguard, who wore expensive shoes and smelled of perfume, hovered around the door. I asked Kishore about the state of Indian politics. The main problem, he said, was the lack of national unity. Appeasement of the Muslims was a threat, and so was the US, which was scheming to make India fall apart, like the Soviet Union. I asked him about the Ram temple. It would be built in two years' time, he said. If not, the VHP would "agitate." I inquired what that might involve. He closed his eyes and remained silent for a while. Then, all of a sudden, he said something astonishing: "The solution to the Muslim problem is simple. The white men, the Hindus, and the Israelis must get together, and we will take care of the Muslim problem once and for all."

In fact, no one is allowed to build anything on the site of the destroyed Babri Masjid. Hindu activists of the

VHP, or the paramilitary RSS, are banned from the area.[8] And to avoid further trouble, the central government bought the land. Absurdly, it has been left to the High Court in Delhi to sort out who has more claim to the holy place, Hindus or Muslims. Lawyers will have to ponder whether the legendary Ram was really born there, whether there ever was a Hindu temple, and exactly what Babur did in 1528. Possibly, there never will be a verdict, which would suit the government just fine. Meanwhile worshipers are allowed to pay their respects to an idol of Ram, located in an improvised shrine on top of the demolished mosque. And hundreds of workmen in Ayodhya, paid by the VHP, are chiseling and carving away at expensive blocks of pink Rajasthani stone for a Ram temple that may never be built. "It is all political," said a local journalist, who took me around. "They want to show the Hindus that work is in progress."

At present the site is like an armed fortress. First you have to get through two police roadblocks. Then you wend your way through a steel cage, guarded by armed constabulary officers, past more checkpoints, until you get to the shrine, which you can just see through iron bars and barbed wire. The shrine, containing Ram and Hanuman, the monkey god, is surrounded by policemen. Worshipers are told to keep moving on. No one is able to linger. A bank of ten television monitors covers every entrance. One was out of order. A monkey

---

8. RSS stands for the Rashtriya Swayamsevali Sargh, or National Volunteer Corps.

had bitten through the wire. I later thought of this scene when I visited the temples of democracy in Chandigarh. The irony seemed perfect: rationalism and religion, modernity and tradition, Corbu's temples and Ram's shrine, all of them under armed guard, all for political show.

And yet the neat juxtaposition would be misleading. For Hindu nationalism is as modern as Nehru's secular idea of India. In a way, Ayodhya and Chandigarh are two sides of a single coin. The most exhaustive book on Hindu nationalism is *The Hindu Nationalist Movement in India*, by the French scholar Christophe Jaffrelot.[9] It is perhaps too exhaustive for the non-specialist, who will be overwhelmed by detail. But it is a scholarly tour de force, and Jaffrelot's argument is clear enough. Hindu nationalism is neither ancient nor religious; it is a political phenomenon which started in the 1920s, when Indian intellectuals were wrestling with ideas of the Indian nation. A key text, quoted by Jaffrelot, is V. D. Savarkar's *Hindutva: Who Is a Hindu?*, published in 1923. Savarkar was inspired by Mazzini, Darwin, and Herbert Spencer. But his main inspiration was fear—fear that the "weak," diverse, disunited Hindus, who lacked an ideology, a dogma, a

---

9. Columbia University Press, 1997. There are others. At least two good books are available in the US: B. D. Graham, *Hindu Nationalism and Indian Politics* (Cambridge University Press, 1990), and P. van der Veer, *Religious Nationalism: Hindus and Muslims in India* (University of California Press, 1994). The Ayodhya affair is also discussed in Stanley J. Tambiah, *Levelling Crowds: Ethnonationalist Conflicts and Collective Violence in South Asia* (University of California Press, 1996).

Mecca, or a universal church, would be swamped by "strong" Muslims and Christians. This fear is still at the core of Hindu nationalism today. That is why VHP demagogues in 1992 promised to purge Ayodhya of Muslims and make it the Hindu Vatican.

Savarkar, like many European thinkers who used religion to concoct national identities, was not a pious man himself. But he thought Hindu rituals and pilgrimages were useful "from a national and racial point of view." Ram, the idol of worship in Ayodhya, is not worshiped as a deity by all Hindus. Only the Vaishnavas—the followers of Vishnu, of whom Ram is an incarnation—do so. But to Savarkar and his modern followers Ram is the symbolic king of the Hindus, the father of the nation. "Some of us," he wrote, "worship Ram as an incarnation, some admire him as a hero and a warrior, all love him as the most illustrious representative monarch of our race."[10]

Unlike Gandhi, who used the imagery of village India to challenge the British Raj, Hindu nationalists imitated the symbols of British power. The RSS, founded in 1925 as a paramilitary Hindu sect, drilled its youngsters, dressed in khaki shorts, to British martial music. Most Hindu nationalists were of high castes. Their idea of India was as a powerful, upper-caste Hindu nation. Gandhi wanted to emancipate the untouchables and protect the Muslims. This was enough reason for a Hindu fanatic with a fascination for Savarkar to assassinate him.

---

10. Quoted in Tapan Basu et al., *Khaki Shorts and Saffron Flags* (New Delhi: Orient Longman, 1993).

Indian political debates during the last decades of the British Empire were not so different from those taking place in Europe, or China, or Japan. Should a modern nation-state be secular, democratic, and ethnically neutral, or should it "reflect" a unified culture, religion, or race? Hindu chauvinism has often been compared to fascism, or even Nazism. Jaffrelot shows how some important Hindu ideologues admired Hitler, and were inspired by German ideas. He quotes the RSS guru, M. S. Golwalkar:

> To keep up the purity of the Race and its culture, Germany shocked the world by her purging the country of the semitic Races—the Jews. Race pride at its highest has been manifested here. Germany has also shown how well nigh impossible it is for Races and cultures, having differences going to the root, to be assimilated into one united whole, a good lesson for us in Hindustan to learn and profit by.

But Jaffrelot warns against simple equations. Hindus rarely made a fetish of blood or race. Rather, they wanted to incorporate all minorities in the Hindu fold. They still do. I saw pictures of Mother Theresa in shrines to Durga, the Mother Goddess. And I was told by a BJP spokesman in Lucknow that since Indian Muslims were converts, Ram was their divine ancestor too. The problem with Muslims has been their refusal to renounce their faith.

3

- - - - -

STILL, FOR AT least thirty years after Independence, Nehru's idea of India prevailed. It was forbidden by law to use religious symbols for electoral purposes. By securing the support for his Congress Party of most high-caste Hindus, including many traditionalists, and of the Muslims, whose interests he tried to protect, he pushed the Hindu chauvinists to the extremist fringe. And the socialists and Communists in opposition shared his secular views. Nonetheless, as Jaffrelot points out, the seeds of future trouble were already planted in 1948, by the Congress Party itself, in Ayodhya. The Congress candidate painted his socialist opponent in a by-election as a materialist lacking in Hindu spiritual values, while presenting himself as a paragon of Hindu orthodoxy. In the following year, Hindu fanatics broke into the Ayodhya mosque and placed an idol of Ram there. Devotees greeted this event as a miracle.

Further dents in Nehru's secular edifice were made by his daughter, Indira, who replaced his *de haut en bas* democracy by what Sunil Khilnani calls "a Jacobin conception of direct popular sovereignty." More and more people began to vote. And to gain their support, Mrs. Gandhi made deals with Sikh separatists, Hindu nationalists, and Muslims, promising state patronage in exchange for votes. Her son Rajiv continued the process. Despite India's secular constitution, Muslims were allowed to retain special marriage laws—to the advantage of Muslim men but not Muslim women, whose rights, after a divorce, are limited. As though to restore the balance, Rajiv kicked off his 1989 election campaign near Ayodhya, because, he declared, it was "the land of Ram, this holy land." And it was Rajiv who gave instruction to unlock the gates of the disputed but defunct Ayodhya mosque, as the first step to a Hindu restoration.

The result of these gestures to communal sentiments was described to me by a weary senior bureaucrat in Lucknow, the capital of Uttar Pradesh, whose confidence in politicians had ebbed with his years in their service. He had a picture of Nehru on his office wall. He said the worst mistake of the Gandhis (mother and son) was to make the Congress Party "play on the same wicket as the BJP." By playing politics with caste and creed, they made Hindu nationalism respectable. So when the Congress monopoly on power collapsed roughly at the end of the cold war,[11] many high-caste Hindu traditionalists transferred their allegiance to the BJP.[12] V. S. Naipaul has described this as a great awakening, a necessary stage in "self-awareness."[13] This might betray a degree of historical naiveté. If anything

11. There is an interesting parallel here with the Liberal Democrats in Japan. Once the monopoly of one party came to an end, its factions split into various parties.

12. This was the trend in northern India. Politics are a different story in southern India, where the Muslim population is much smaller and Brahmin domination has been diminished.

13. See the interview with V. S. Naipaul in *India Today*, August 19, 1997.

was reawakened, it was Sarvarkar's idea of India, which had been so deftly discredited by Nehru.

BJP politics plays on high-caste Hindu fears and frustrations: fear that lower castes, through positive discrimination ("reservations"), will squeeze high-caste Hindus out of overcrowded government jobs; fear that Muslims enjoy unfair privileges, or, by being "backward," keep India weak and poor. Since Muslims and low-caste Hindus are getting politically active, high-caste Hindus feel vulnerable. They sense that their dominance is slipping. What the BJP promises is not so much the restoration of a Hindu Golden Age as a strong, modern Hindu state with Ayodyha as its Vatican. Nothing about this is traditional, or even necessarily antidemocratic. Although the increased importance of communal politics has shaken the faith of some people in India's democracy, Sunil Khilnani is not one of them. He writes, again, I think, with wisdom:

> Regional and caste politics, and Hindu nationalism, embody different potentialities, but they are all direct products of India's first four decades of independence. It is wrong to see them as atavistic forms that repudiate or attack the ideas of the state and democracy; on the contrary, they exemplify the triumphant success of these ideas.

But what of his other argument, about the civilizing process of constitutional democracy? Destroying mosques and killing Muslims is hardly civilized behavior. The current level of violence is nothing compared to the carnage that took place during Partition, but it has been steadily rising since the 1950s. The reaction to the violence in Ayodhya has been interesting, however. Even the BJP leaders appear to have been shocked by what they had set in motion, if not actively organized. Advani, and others, were arrested by the central government for inciting communal violence. Public disapproval ran so high that the BJP did badly in the 1993 state elections of Uttar Pradesh. As a result, the BJP was forced to share the state government with the BSP (Bahujan Samaj Party), a party of Dalits, the lowest caste. The BSP is led by the forty-one-year-old Mrs. Mayawati, a Dalit herself.[14] This peculiar alliance, of high castes and the very lowest, alternating in power every six months, was based on their shared dislike of a third party, the SP (Samajwadi Party), which represents the "other backward classes" (OBCs). These other low castes have increasingly moved out of dire poverty by becoming small landowners, businessmen, and civil servants. Many policemen are OBCs. So are most of the thugs who beat up Muslims or, indeed, Dalits.[15]

A short walk around my hotel in Lucknow revealed something about the present state of India, or at least of its Hindi belt. There was a general air of national assertion, with a hint of aggression. Outside the hotel entrance was a large new statue of Subhas Chandra

---

14. The current president of India, K. R. Narayanan, is also a Dalit.

15. One of the most disturbing and entertaining descriptions of the upwardly mobile classes in provincial India is in Pankaj Mishra, *Butter Chicken in Ludhiana: Travels in Small Town India* (Penguin India, 1995).

Bose, the militant Bengali nationalist who allied himself to the Imperial Japanese army during the war. His picture can often be seen in VHP and RSS offices. Bose was one of those men whose idea of nationhood was based on military discipline and the *Führerprinzip*. There he stands, the rotund tough guy, in his jackboots and his uniform, a strutting reproach to the gentler Gandhi and the brooding Anglophile Nehru.

Behind the statue of Bose, I examined the billboards advertising computer courses, schools, and consumer products: "Totally modern, totally Indian." A college, promising bright career prospects, advertised itself by saying: "Be Indian, stay Indian. Now go for an education that is totally Indian—with us." Under the billboards was a slum of terrifying poverty: hovels made of rags, black with grime; children with copper-colored hair, caused by malnutrition, played in the rubbish, where men were defecating. They were Dalits.

The assertion of national identity was striking, but the assertion of caste identity was even more so. One of the first things Mrs. Mayawati did as chief minister of Uttar Pradesh was to build statues of B.R. Ambedkar, the leader of the "untouchables." Ambedkar, shown as a bespectacled figure pointing, Lenin-like, to a better future, was of the lowest caste himself. As Nehru's law minister in 1947, he helped to frame the national constitution, which outlawed caste discrimination. But he was so disillusioned by the lack of actual progress that he resigned from politics and became a Buddhist. During the six months of Mrs. Mayawati's rule, Ambedkar suddenly appeared everywhere, in Lucknow, in

"Ambedkar villages" around Lucknow, and indeed all over Uttar Pradesh. The demand for Ambedkar statues was so pressing that there were not enough sculptors to go round. A large bronze Ambedkar now stands in the center of Lucknow, opposite an older, more modest-sized Gandhi.

Inside the back of Ambedkar's statue is a heavily guarded police box. "Security problems," I was told. Ashok Priyadarshi, the secretary to the Uttar Pradesh government, took me to see Mrs. Mayawati's grandest project: Ambedkar Park. On the way he explained that Mrs. Mayawati had changed the political scene in U. P. forever. The statues and the Ambedkar villages may look like nothing but gestures, but they amount to more than that. The Dalits have woken up. They will assert their power through the ballot box. He told me this in the neutral style of a civil servant. But when we drove past Ambedkar Park, a huge building site with skeletons of fantastic, modern buildings in pink and white stone, his manner changed. He shook his head sadly, and said: "All that money. Where did it all come from? Who will account for it? All that corruption, that is there..." Mr. Priyadarshi was not even sure what the buildings were for. One was to be an international hotel, he thought, and another, well, a science institute maybe?

Perhaps we will never know. In October, the BJP took its turn to govern U. P. Instantly government jobs started going to BJP supporters. Dalits were officially warned not to "abuse" the laws that protected them against caste discrimination. Mrs. Mayawati was accused of corruption. Some members of her party defected. Violent scenes followed in the state legislature. Politicians pelted each other with chairs, microphones, inkstands, or whatever else came to hand. Some ended up in the hospital. The central government was asked to dissolve the unruly government of Uttar Pradesh and impose presidential rule. Despite fierce opposition from regional parties in the government, it agreed to do so. But when the President asked the Cabinet to reconsider, the decision was reversed. The BJP called this a great day for democracy. But it was a bad day for Prime Minister I.K. Gujral's shaky coalition government in Delhi. The debacle exposed divisions in the central government, which are as deep as those which tore apart the state government of U.P.

I called Mr. Priyardashi to ask him what was going on now in Ambedkar Park. Building was slowly coming to a halt, he said. It is now "subject to enquiry," he said. "Massive bungling," he said. "Many heads will roll," he said. He didn't sound overly disturbed. He had seen it all before.

NOVEMBER 6, 1997

Christopher de Bellaigue

- - - - -

BOMBAY AT WAR

1

- - - - -

ONCE INDIA HAD a liberal city called Bombay.
Its businessmen were cannier than those of the rest
of socialist India, its rich more cosmopolitan, its
cricketers more flamboyant. Bombay's was a relatively
pluralistic tradition, too. In faraway Calcutta, India's
British colonizers had spent the nineteenth century
creating a paternalistic seat of empire with heavy-
handed imitations of English buildings. In Bombay,
on the other hand, prosperous native businessmen col-
laborated with their foreign masters to create a port
city whose architecture amalgamated, with appropriate symbolism, European and Indian styles. Well into
the 1990s it was possible to explain, as many did, the
incidence of the city's poverty and corruption as the natural concomitants of Bombay's commercial dynamism.
Compared with other places on the subcontinent, India's
most complex city, its window on the world, was still
considered a fine place to be.

Now, India has an ugly, disturbing shrine city called
Mumbai. It is a Hindu shrine, since the diverse, generally tolerant religion practiced by four out of five

Indians has acquired a venomous political identity in the very city where religious minorities like the Muslims, the Jains, and the Parsees have tended to do best. Officially, Bombay turned into Mumbai in 1996, when the Hindu nationalist government of the state of Maharashtra decided to rename the state capital in the Marathi vernacular. But the context for this semantic shuffle was a rejection of the secular, universalist values espoused by Mohandas K. Gandhi and Jawaharlal Nehru. To many residents of India's commercial capital, Mumbai was born at the moment that this rejection reached its climax: December 6, 1992.

That was the day that Hindu chauvinists defied the central government in Delhi and tore down the Babri Mosque, a north Indian mosque that had been built, Hindus believe, on the site of the birthplace of Rama, a revered deity. The mosque's destruction gave rise to bloody fighting between Hindus and Muslims in towns across north India. Despite lying 750 miles southwest of the Babri Mosque, Bombay was the worst affected. For five days that December and fifteen days the following month, intercommunal rioting between Hindus and Muslims cost the lives of some 900 people in Bombay, two thirds of them from the Muslim minority community and more than 350 of them killed by the security forces. Barely a month later, ten explosions, allegedly the work of Dawood Ibrahim, the city's top Muslim gang boss—"Mumbai's Al Capone"—evened the score. The final toll: 1,217 dead, 2,036 injured.

Even now, many Mumbaikars wonder how their city could have succumbed to a sectarian nationalism that is anathema to its traditional mercantile sophistication. After all, the millions who immigrate here do so in search of rupees: from the upstate migrants churning out T-shirts in suburban sweatshops to Tamil entrepreneurs bent over the ledgers of compact little businesses; from the eunuch prostitutes touting for business in Falkland Road to the north Indian Muslims manning the fruit stalls of Bhendi Bazaar. Six years after the riots, it may look like business as usual on the narrow, tense thoroughfare that divides a Muslim-majority district from its predominantly Hindu neighbor. But not since thousands followed the quintessential Bombay Muslim, Muhammad Ali Jinnah, when he left India to become Pakistan's first governor general in 1947 has communal identity in the city been so self-conscious. In the fashionable apartment blocks of south Mumbai, well-heeled Hindus may wish their affluent Muslim neighbors *Eid Mubarak* at the end of Ramadan, but you will look in vain for a Khan, a Khoreishi, or an Ansari among the brass nameplates on lobby walls. Removed by Muslims fearful for their lives during the riots, they have yet to be replaced. "On the surface everything seems normal," says one Koran-seller, "but we are seething."

2

- - - - -

THE CAMPAIGN TO dismantle the Babri Mosque was not a new one; nor was its chief political proponent, the Bharatiya Janata Party (BJP), a particularly original variant on the handful of Hindu nationalist parties that have been part of India's political landscape since Independence. By the late 1980s, however, the conditions had arisen that would allow Hindu nationalism to shift to the center of India's political life. Nehru's Congress Party was committed to redistribution of wealth and reducing caste privilege, but it was exhausted by more than forty years of almost uninterrupted power and had grown corrupt and brittle. A nascent Hindu middle class, patriotic and devout, rejected the Congress and other parties of the left as beholden to the lower castes and religious minorities. After Pakistan-backed Muslims in disputed Jammu and Kashmir stepped up their violent campaign for self-determination, the BJP emerged as a champion of both Indian military superiority and high-caste Hindu thrift. It combined woolly themes like self-sufficiency with fierce belligerence on the mosque issue and toward Pakistan. Still, it took a full five years after the Babri Mosque fell before the BJP finally shed its political untouchability. Only after last year's parliamentary elections, when the BJP emerged the strongest party in Delhi's parliament, did Atal Bihari Vajpayee, the party leader, succeed in forming the coalition government that currently runs India.

A little over a year later, Mr. Vajpayee's job is looking tougher than ever. In particular, the prime minister is having difficulty explaining to his more secular-minded coalition partners the BJP's enduring links with several shady, neofascist Hindu organizations. In January, for example, an outcry both at home and

abroad forced him to order a judicial inquiry into
the deaths of an Australian Christian missionary and
his two children, allegedly at the hands of one such
group, the Bajrang Dal. But for the political relationship that most embarrasses the prime minister, we must
look back to Mumbai, to India's least amiable dema-
gogue: Balasaheb K. Thackeray, a sometime political
cartoonist who decided to go into politics and succeeded beyond expectations.

When Mr. Thackeray founded his Shiv Sena party
in 1966, he reckoned that the name of Shivaji—a
seventeenth-century king from modern-day Maharashtra, who won striking military successes against Muslim
invaders—would give added support to his campaign
against the south Indians who exerted such influence
over the Mumbai economy. By the mid-1980s, however, Mr. Thackeray had decisively associated his ailing
party with the rising power of Hindu nationalism and
the same warrior king became synonymous with
another sort of bigotry. By then, the Shiv Sena had
acquired a reputation as a kind of sectarian Salvation
Army, providing social services for Hindus of different
castes. But Mr. Thackeray's 40,000 *sainiks*—his warriors, who are expected to have the disciplined dedication that the word implies—proved to be adept
brownshirts, too. According to the findings of an independent inquiry conducted by B. N. Shrikrishna, a High
Court judge (and devout Hindu), the Shiv Sena "took
the lead in organizing attacks on Muslims" during the
1992–1993 riots. As for Mr. Thackeray, he "commanded
his loyal *Shiv Sainiks* . . . like a veteran general."

The Shiv Sena bloodied its hands, but Mr. Thackeray's change of emphasis worked; he went from a bit player to the dominant personality in Maharashtran politics. In the 1995 assembly elections, the Shiv Sena confidently joined forces with the BJP and captured the state government from a jaded and discredited Congress. No matter that some BJP leaders, especially those in Mr. Vajpeyee's government, now regard Mr. Thackeray as an embarrassment; although they rebuke him, they have not dared to ditch him, for the BJP's electoral prospects in Maharashtra would suffer without the Shiv Sena's support. As for the Shiv Sena leader himself, he holds no office in the state government, but boasts of running Maharashtra extra-constitutionally from his well-guarded house in the suburbs. An inveterate braggart, on such occasions he is not exaggerating.

A good illustration of the power exerted by this well-connected artist—at least one US diplomatic envoy has sat for him—was provided this January, when Mr. Thackeray successfully demanded the resignation of Manohar Joshi, Maharashtra's chief minister since 1995. According to some political analysts in Mumbai, the outgoing chief minister had fallen from favor by failing to make good on a series of ambitious Shiv Sena promises: free housing for four million Mumbai slum dwellers and free electricity for farmers in different parts of the state. The latter was a pledge the excitable Mr. Thackeray had made without consulting his minister of power.

Ask BJP members of the government, however, and they will tell you that Mr. Thackeray was determined to punish Mr. Joshi for doing nothing to prevent the arrest of fourteen *sainiks* discovered ransacking the headquarters of India's cricket board in protest over the Delhi government's refusal to cancel a test series against Pakistan—a sporting encounter that Hindu nationalists found offensive, in view of Pakistan's claims to Kashmir. Whatever the cause, it is unlikely that Mr. Joshi's departure had anything to do with his being implicated in an official investigation into the illegal allotment of a chunk of public land. After all, his swiftly appointed successor, Narayan Rane, was once named by police as a conspirator in the murder of an opposition Congress Party worker. State cabinet ministers like Pramod Navalkar smile bleakly when asked about Mr. Joshi's departure. "We are the last to know the reason for such things," he told me. "We are loyal only to Mr. Thackeray and we accept what he says." And there he stopped. One of Mr. Rane's first actions as chief minister has been to instruct his ministers to keep away from the press.

For all Mr. Thackeray's impatience with Mr. Joshi, the outgoing chief minister—who departed with the pious assertion that he had fallen on his sword "like a disciplined *sainik*"—was generous to his boss. Mr. Joshi saw to it that a large number of criminal and civil suits filed against Mr. Thackeray and other senior *sainiks* were dropped; he scrapped the State Minorities Commission—a statutory body given to needling the Shiv Sena—and publicly denounced the findings of the Shrikrishna report. Even though the report identifies in Mumbai's 38,000-strong police force "an inbuilt bias against the Muslims," all but one of the officers it accuses of crimes like "looting . . . rioting" and "utter dereliction of duty" during the riots remain on the beat.

In common with other neofascist parties, the Sena thrives on political agitations that often take the form of mass protests. Perhaps inevitably, four years of power have blunted the party's ability to disrupt. It can no longer organize citywide strikes that were once exhilarating to their Sena followers. Nevertheless, the Shiv Sena can still have fun in the guise of guardian of public morals, particularly when it targets independent-minded filmmakers from Bollywood, the city's influential movie industry.

With an output of some 120 films a year, Bollywood contributes heavily to the Mumbai economy. Nevertheless, its power did not stop Mr. Thackeray last year when he organized attacks by (mostly female) *sainiks* on one of two Mumbai theaters that were showing *Fire*, Bollywood's first exploration of lesbian romance —which the Shiv Sena leader denounced as "alien to Indian culture." The police were nowhere to be seen when Mr. Thackeray's acolytes smashed windows and tore down posters at the Cinemax Theatre, where the film was playing to a packed house; nor were they when similar attacks took place the following day in three more Indian cities. In Mumbai, New Delhi, Pune, and Surat, *Fire*'s run came to an enforced end.

The Sena does not, however, need such violence to collect more money. When the Mumbai-based *Times of India* introduced forty-five-year-old Mr. Rane, a teeto-taling ex–bar owner, to its readers, the paper drew flattering attention to the new chief minister's "ability to raise funds for the party." When I talked with lesser *sainiks* in Mumbai this winter, it soon became clear that the Shiv Sena is extremely good at persuading Mumbai businessmen to pay for the merry-go-round of rallies, religious spectacles, and extravagant shows of philanthropy that have demonstrably tied the party to Mumbai public life. "Not *hapta*, you understand, but *dan*." Not extortion, but donations. One talkative resident of a Shiv Sena–controlled district disagreed. "Businessmen where I come from are told to pay up to $25,000 if one of the big festivals is being planned." According to one former member of that now defunct minorities commission, "The reason why certain Muslim-owned hardware stores in central Mumbai were not attacked during the riots is that their owners had paid protection money to the Shiv Sena."

Whatever the fund-raising methods used by Mr. Rane, taxi drivers working the blue-chip route into Mumbai from the city's domestic airport fear that his appointment will increase the amount they have to pay the party—especially in the months before next spring's assembly elections. Nevertheless, it would be unfair to portray the Shiv Sena as the only recipient of untaxed rupees in Mumbai, still less as the sole reason why middle- and upper-class Mumbaikars have come to fear for their wealth. The other specialists in menacing people for money are a group which has thrived in connivance with cooperative politicians, policemen, and, latterly, cash-strapped Bollywood producers: the Mumbai mob.

Spend a little time in Mumbai and it seems appropriate that it should have earned a reputation as India's hard currency laundromat; this, after all, is the sort of place where millionaires with offshore accounts encourage the exteriors of their sumptuously appointed apartments to crumble, the better to escape the attentions of gangsters and tax inspectors. Before the Congress government of the early 1990s nudged India into piecemeal free trade policies, Mumbai's underworld survived on the proceeds from sales of smuggled Scotch and gold. Blade-toting "brothers"—the dons, in local parlance—competed to intimidate the throneholders of the "license permit Raj," a labyrinthine system of patronage in which hugely profitable stakes in local industries were effectively auctioned to cronyish conglomerates. According to the police, once tariff reductions had slashed the profitability of these pursuits, the attention of dons like Mr. Ibrahim and Arun Gawli, a lesser rival, turned to the international trade in Pakistan-produced heroin. Even then, though, the Mafia remained at one remove from the lives of most normal citizens. The 1993 bomb blasts changed that.

The explosions that half-gutted Mumbai landmarks like the stock exchange and Air India buildings heralded the split into factions, along Hindu–Muslim lines, of the city's hitherto secular-minded underworld. When the police announced that they had found Karachi markings on the packages used for transporting the explosives responsible for the blasts, Mr. Ibrahim—well known as the top Mafia boss and already regarded as an avenging angel by terrorized

Mumbai Muslims—was branded a Pakistani agent, and accused of running his narcotics ring in partnership with Pakistan's secret service. Hindu lieutenants of Mr. Ibrahim broke away to form rival "loyalist" gangs. Meanwhile, the soaring price of prime residential and commercial property in south Mumbai had encouraged the brothers to take up speculation. According to Shiv Anandan, a joint police commissioner, Bollywood, too, "has been completely infiltrated by crime." No wonder the gangs are in the midst of a grand turf war.

The war has not merely affected the dons, their immediate entourage, and a handful of crooked businessmen. In humble Muslim neighborhoods like Nagpada, where Mr. Ibrahim's sister lives and Ibrahim men collect the *dan*, unemployed Muslim youths readily deliver packages of heroin for ten dollars, a princely sum; a trash-picker living in one of Mumbai's 40,000-odd *chawls*, the one-room tenements built to serve workers in the inner city's now defunct textile mills, might slit a tenant's throat for little more than one hundred dollars. What is more, the murderer could well be risking capital punishment merely to settle a dispute over the right to occupy a miserable flat.

To the police, the pattern is familiar. Thanks to Mumbai's anachronistic rent controls, rents of as little as five dollars per month are not unknown for the kind of apartment that has a market value of $750,000. Not surprisingly, in such cases, the landlord generally wants his tenant evicted. According to a senior Mumbai policeman, "Rather than wait fifteen years [the time it would take for his eviction suit to reach Mumbai's logjammed courts], the frustrated landlord might ask the brothers to get rid of the tenant." Meanwhile, the terrified wives of Mumbai's millionaires have begun wearing "American" (fake) jewelry to the season's fanciest weddings. And once the driver has parked the family Mercedes outside the colonial-era club hired for the event, a fee will change hands to ensure that it escapes "modification."

This, then, is the Mumbai of the 1990s. It would be easy to shovel all the responsibility for its grim evolution onto Bal Thackeray. But even when it comes to relations between Hindus and Muslims, this would not be accurate. In December 1992 and January 1993, after all, gutless and opportunistic Congress governments were in control in both New Delhi and Mumbai. Now, in Chagan Bhujbal, the Congress Party in Maharashtra has a leader who not only rose to prominence as one of Mr. Thackeray's most outspoken *sainiks*, but once introduced such spleen into a speech on minorities that the speaker of the assembly ordered his obscenities expunged from the record.

Equally, state Congress leaders share—along with the Shiv Sena—responsibility for Mumbai's flourishing criminal culture. The rot set in under the previous, more subtly pro-Hindu Congress government. Even now, Mumbai police say that brothers like Arun Gawli (not to mention his political party) have been supported by senior Congress politicians. Likewise, it is worth recalling the role played by Mumbai's conservative Islamic clergy in the emergence, since the riots, of a sullen isolationism among Mumbai Muslims, whether Sunni,

Shi'ite, or members of the heterodox Bohri community. From record numbers of Mecca-bound pilgrims to the prospering trade in *burqas*—the all-concealing garb that forcefully symbolizes a woman's submission to the tenets of the Koran—the prevailing religiosity does not bode well for hopes of a revival of religious tolerance.

47

Nor can the Shiv Sena be entirely blamed for the recent downturn in Mumbai's economy. Foreign investors have been scared off by criminality and the Sena's sharply nationalistic rhetoric, but a sharp dip in most Indian GNP growth projections is also responsible. Nor is Mr. Thackeray exclusively responsible for the plight of the city's slum dwellers—some 4.5 million out of a population of around 11 million. True, his scheme to provide land for commercial development to those who were also prepared to build housing for the poor collapsed along with property prices in 1997. But the record of previous Congress governments was little better. The best way of upgrading slums—transfer the deeds to the slum dwellers themselves, giving them an incentive to improve their own housing—presents complicated legal obstacles and therefore little opportunity for short-term electoral benefit. It also denies property magnates the chance to develop the land in question for commercial use and so runs into powerful opposition. In the late 1980s, some 22,000 families obtained title deeds for land on which they were squatting, but this scheme was discontinued well before the Shiv Sena came to power.

Still, it is hard to find an aspect of Mumbai's civic life that the Shiv Sena has changed for the better, or a problem it has not—often willfully—made worse.

Since successive central governments in New Delhi have declined to dismiss the Maharashtra government, it falls to those liberal-minded, articulate Mumbaikars —the city's cultural elite, and its more enlightened industrialists—to lead a countercharge against the communalists and the brothers. What are these people doing?

3

- - - - -

ONE WAY TO answer this question is to take the Juhu Road north from the island city, past pristine Chowpatty Beach, its new cleanliness a rare instance of administrative competence, past Shivaji Park—where Sachin Tendulkar, nowadays reckoned the finest cricketer in the world, played as a boy, and where Mr. Thackeray addresses his supporters in whimsical Marathi. Clear Mumbai's international airport and its dank surrounds of slum and *chawl*, and you have reached Mumbai's—and therefore India's—most visible symbol of liberal-minded hedonism. If you have read Shobha De's novel *Starry Nights*, you will know something about the heady life of the world's most prolific movie industry. This is its headquarters: Bollywood.

Every day, around ten million Indians buy a movie ticket. In 1996, when a public television channel showed *Sholay* (*The Flames*), the most famous Bollywood movie of all, some quarter of a billion Indians watched. Such statistics illustrate the fascination that the movies exert

over Indians—a hold rivaled only by cricket. Bollywood's favorite genre is the musical melodrama, in
which the heroine, her sari often tantalizingly soaked
by an unseasonal shower, is rescued by her muscular
beau, accompanied by a thunderous score. By popular-
izing the Hindi language, Bollywood has helped to
unify India's multilingual society, all the while addressing a diaspora which extends from Toronto to Kuala
Lumpur. Not surprisingly, when Bollywood speaks, the
rest of India listens.

It has interesting things to say, too. Bollywood has,
to an extent unthinkable in other parts of Indian life,
dispensed with the traditional preoccupation with caste
and religious identity. At present, three male leads can
command the colossal sum of $300,000 per picture; all
are Pathan Muslims surnamed Khan. From the veteran
Dilip Kumar to character actors like Naseeruddin Shah
and Shabana Azmi, Bollywood is hugely indebted to
Muslim talent. (Too indebted, whispers Shobha De, a
convent-educated Brahman who suspects the industry
of an Islamic conspiracy.) Even M. F. Hussein, India's
immensely popular Muslim painter, is currently making
his maiden movie. Mr. Hussein does not seem like someone who would be intimidated by the chauvinists; his
nude representation of Saraswati, the Hindu goddess of
wisdom, was once burned by them. Rallying behind a
celebrity like Mr. Hussein, you might think that the Bollywood leaders could take on the Shiv Sena, and even win.

In fact, they don't. The gap between such expectations and reality are neatly illustrated by the fate of a
petition protesting the Shiv Sena's violent response to

Fire and signed by a handful of big Bollywood names. Ms. Azmi, the film's heroine, praised the petition as "very significant." But the outspoken few have received very little support from their peers. When the house of Mr. Kumar, one of the signers, was surrounded by hostile *sainiks* wearing nothing but their underpants—a gesture designed to underscore the film's immodesty—the actor's only support was "some sporadic telephone calls adding up to not very much." Mahesh Bhatt, a director who signed the petition, describes the reaction of other Bollywood big shots as one of "apathy and cowardice."

For an illustration of the servility with which Bollywood has bowed to a philosophy inimical to its own, consider the January opening of a much-hyped show of political caricatures by Raj Thackeray, the nephew of the Shiv Sena leader and a potential heir to the throne. Exhaustively promoted by the supposedly secular-minded *Times of India*, which devoted three laudatory articles—each more craven than the last—to the exhibition, the show was lent luster by the presence of some of the biggest names in Bollywood. Amitabh Bacchan, star of *Sholay* and probably the most revered living Indian; Madhuri Dixit, the quintessential Bollywood siren in the 1990s; and Shobha De, the Western press's favorite liberated Indian female—all were there. Most noteworthy of all, however, was the presence of M. F. Hussein, whose portrait of Saraswati had been torched by Hindu nationalists. No wonder Mr. Hussein is regarded as something of a turncoat among the Muslims of Bombay.

The Thackeray exhibition illustrates an important truth about Mumbai. From US-educated industrialists to the most urbane of Bollywood stars, the elite of the city has decided that it pays to get on with the Shiv Sena. Few of Mumbai's powerful conglomerates have dared to fall out publicly with the Hindu chauvinists. Javed Akhtar, a Bollywood lyric-writer and Urdu poet, likens Bollywood's reluctance to confront the Shiv Sena to the reaction of a frog dropped into a pan of water on a stove. "If the water is boiling, the frog will naturally leap out," he says. "But put the frog into cold water and turn on the stove, and you end up with poached frog."

Still, there are signs that Maharashtran voters in general may be getting fed up. In last year's general election, they gave the Shiv Sena and the BJP a beating, returning just ten Hindu nationalist deputies from a total of forty-eight constituencies across the state—a significant dip from the thirty-four held by the Shiv Sena and BJP in the previous parliament. More encouraging still, Mr. Thackeray's posturing against the Pakistani cricket tour and the screening of *Fire* were poorly received by many Mumbaikars, who take a dim view of political interference in their two chief passions. In March of 2000, when Maharashtrans elect a new state assembly, the chauvinists may well be out on their ear. With the Congress's Mr. Bhujbal waiting in the wings, it seems unlikely that Mumbai will regain its former reputation as a socially cohesive city. A spell in opposition might even revitalize the Shiv Sena. In the meantime, the party is busy bleeding the city dry, as the traditions of tolerance and respect for the rule of law—

essential if a place of this complexity is to survive and prosper—become quaint reminders of the past.

In some ways, Mumbai has lost its special status, laid low by problems of corruption and religious antagonism that afflict the rest of India. As the country embarks on its second half-century of independent life, the decline of the Congress and the receptivity of voters to Hindu majoritarianism has helped produce a set of politicians altogether different from one-nation secularists like Jawaharlal Nehru. In Bal Thackeray, Maharashtra has a state boss as unattractive as any other; in its Mafia, it has the most powerful criminal elite in Southeast Asia. As long as such men as these continue to stifle Mumbai's traditional mercantile egalitarianism, there is little likelihood that much will change. If, however, liberal politics and responsible economics can somehow emerge—a very big "if"—the city would be ideally placed to lead an Indian recovery.

MARCH 24, 1999

Amartya Sen

- - - - -

TAGORE

AND

HIS INDIA

RABINDRANATH TAGORE, WHO died in 1941 at the age of eighty, is a towering figure in the millennium-old literature of Bengal. Anyone who becomes familiar with this large and flourishing tradition will be impressed by the power of Tagore's presence in Bangladesh and in India. His poetry as well as his novels, short stories, and essays are very widely read, and the songs he composed reverberate around the eastern part of India and throughout Bangladesh.

In contrast, in the rest of the world, especially in Europe and America, the excitement that Tagore's writings created in the early years of this century has largely vanished. The enthusiasm with which his work was once greeted was quite remarkable. *Gitanjali*, a selection of his poetry for which he was awarded the Nobel Prize in literature in 1913, was published in English translation in London in March of that year and had been reprinted ten times by November, when the award was announced. But he is not much read now in the West, and already by 1937, Graham Greene was able to say: "As for Rabindranath Tagore, I cannot believe that anyone but Mr. Yeats can still take his poems very seriously."

The contrast between Tagore's commanding presence in Bengali literature and culture and his near-total eclipse in the rest of the world is perhaps less interesting than the distinction between the view of Tagore as a deeply relevant and many-sided contemporary thinker in Bangladesh and India, and his image in the West as a repetitive and remote spiritualist. Graham Greene had, in fact, gone on to explain that he associated Tagore "with what Chesterton calls 'the bright pebbly eyes' of the Theosophists." Certainly, an air of mysticism played some part in the "selling" of Rabindranath Tagore to the West by Yeats, Pound, and his other early champions. Even Anna Akhmatova, one of Tagore's few later admirers (who translated his poems into Russian in the mid-1960s), talks of "that mighty flow of poetry which takes its strength from Hinduism as from the Ganges, and is called Rabindranath Tagore."

Rabindranath did come from a Hindu family—one of the landed gentry who owned estates mostly in what is now Bangladesh. But whatever wisdom there might be in Akhmatova's invoking of Hinduism and the Ganges, it did not prevent the largely Muslim citizens of Bangladesh from having a deep sense of identity with Tagore and his ideas. Nor did it stop the newly independent Bangladesh from choosing one of Tagore's songs ("Amar Sonar Bangla," which means "My Golden Bengal") as its national anthem. This must be very confusing to those who see the contemporary world as a "clash of civilizations"—with "the Muslim civilization,"

"the Hindu civilization," and "the Western civilization," each forcefully confronting the others.

They would also be confused by Rabindranath
Tagore's own description of his Bengali family as the
product of "a confluence of three cultures, Hindu,
Mohammedan and British."[1] Rabindranath's grandfather, Dwarkanath, was well known for his command
of Arabic and Persian, and Rabindranath grew up in
a family atmosphere in which a deep knowledge of
Sanskrit and ancient Hindu texts was combined with
an understanding of Islamic traditions as well as
Persian literature. It is not so much that Rabindranath
tried to produce—or had an interest in producing—
a "synthesis" of the different religions (as the great
Moghul emperor Akbar tried hard to achieve) as that
his outlook was persistently nonsectarian, and his writings—some two hundred books—show the influence of
different parts of the Indian cultural background as
well as of the rest of the world.[2] Most of his work was
written at Santiniketan (Abode of Peace), the small town
that grew around the school he founded in Bengal in
1901. He not only conceived there an imaginative and

1. Rabindranath Tagore, *The Religion of Man* (London: Unwin, 1931, sec-
ond edition, 1961), p. 105. The extensive interactions between Hindu and
Muslim parts of Indian culture (in religious beliefs, civic codes, painting,
sculpture, literature, music, and astronomy) have been discussed by Kshiti
Mohan Sen in *Bharate Hindu Mushalmaner Jukto Sadhana* (in Bengali)
(Calcutta: Visva-Bharati, 1949, extended edition, 1990) and *Hinduism*
(Penguin, 1960).

2. Rabindranath's father, Debendranath, had in fact joined the reformist religious group, the Brahmo Samaj, which rejected many contemporary Hindu
practices as aberrations from the ancient Hindu texts.

innovative system of education—to which I will return —but, through his writings and his influence on students and teachers, he was able to use the school as a base from which he could take a major part in India's social, political, and cultural movements.

The profoundly original writer whose elegant prose and magical poetry Bengali readers know well is not the sermonizing spiritual guru admired—and then rejected—in London. Tagore was not only an immensely versatile poet; he was also a great short-story writer, novelist, playwright, essayist, and composer of songs, as well as a talented painter whose pictures, with their whimsical mixture of representation and abstraction, are only now beginning to receive the acclaim that they have long deserved. His essays, moreover, ranged over literature, politics, culture, social change, religious beliefs, philosophical analysis, international relations, and much else. The coincidence of the fiftieth anniversary of Indian independence with the publication of a selection of Tagore's letters by Cambridge University Press[3] is a good occasion to examine the nature of Tagore's ideas and reflections, and the kind of leadership in thought and understanding he provided in the subcontinent in the first half of this century.

---

3. *Selected Letters of Rabindranath Tagore*, edited by Krishna Dutta and Andrew Robinson (Cambridge University Press, 1997). This essay draws on my Foreword to this collection. For important background material on Rabindranath Tagore and his reception in the West, see also the editors' *Rabindranath Tagore: The Myriad-Minded Man* (St. Martin's, 1995), and *Rabindranath Tagore: An Anthology* (Picador, 1997).

1

- - - - -

GANDHI AND TAGORE

SINCE RABINDRANATH TAGORE and Mohandas Gandhi were two leading Indian thinkers in this century, many commentators have tried to compare their ideas. On learning of Rabindranath's death, Jawaharlal Nehru, then incarcerated in a British jail in India, wrote in his prison diary for August 7, 1941:

> Gandhi and Tagore. Two types entirely different from each other, and yet both of them typical of India, both in the long line of India's great men. . . . It is not so much because of any single virtue but because of the *tout ensemble*, that I felt that among the world's great men today Gandhi and Tagore were supreme as human beings. What good fortune for me to have come into close contact with them.

Romain Rolland was fascinated by the contrast between them, and when he completed his book on Gandhi, he wrote to an Indian academic, in March 1923: "I have finished my *Gandhi*, in which I pay tribute to your two great river-like souls, overflowing with divine spirit, Tagore and Gandhi." The following month he recorded in his diary an account of some of the differences between Gandhi and Tagore written by Reverend C. F. Andrews, the English clergyman and public activist who was a close friend of both men (and whose important role in Gandhi's life in South Africa as well as India is well portrayed in Richard Attenborough's film *Gandhi*). Andrews described to Rolland a discussion between Tagore and Gandhi, at which he was present, on subjects that divided them:

> The first subject of discussion was idols; Gandhi defended them, believing the masses incapable of raising themselves immediately to abstract ideas. Tagore cannot bear to see the people eternally treated as a child. Gandhi quoted the great things achieved in Europe by the flag as an idol; Tagore found it easy to object, but Gandhi held his ground, contrasting European flags bearing eagles, etc., with his own, on which he has put a spinning wheel. The second point of discussion was nationalism, which Gandhi defended. He said that one must go through nationalism to reach internationalism, in the same way that one must go through war to reach peace.[4]

Tagore greatly admired Gandhi but he had many disagreements with him on a variety of subjects, including nationalism, patriotism, the importance of cultural exchange, the role of rationality and of science, and the nature of economic and social development. These differences, I shall argue, have a clear and consis-

---

4. See *Romain Rolland and Gandhi Correspondence*, with a Foreword by Jawaharlal Nehru (New Delhi: Government of India, 1976), pp. 12–13.

tent pattern, with Tagore pressing for more room for reasoning, and for a less traditionalist view, a greater interest in the rest of the world, and more respect for science and for objectivity generally.

Rabindranath knew that he could not have given India the political leadership that Gandhi provided, and he was never stingy in his praise for what Gandhi did for the nation (it was, in fact, Tagore who popularized the term "Mahatma"—great soul—as a description of Gandhi). And yet each remained deeply critical of many things that the other stood for. That Mahatma Gandhi has received incomparably more attention outside India and also within much of India itself makes it important to understand "Tagore's side" of the Gandhi–Tagore debates.

In his prison diary, Nehru wrote: "Perhaps it is as well that [Tagore] died now and did not see the many horrors that are likely to descend in increasing measure on the world and on India. He had seen enough and he was infinitely sad and unhappy." Toward the end of his life, Tagore was indeed becoming discouraged about the state of India, especially as its normal burden of problems, such as hunger and poverty, was being supplemented by politically organized incitement to "communal" violence between Hindus and Muslims. This conflict would lead in 1947, six years after Tagore's death, to the widespread killing that took place during Partition; but there was much gore already during his declining days. In December 1939 he wrote to his friend Leonard Elmhirst, the English philanthropist and social reformer who had worked closely with him on rural reconstruction in India (and who had gone on to found the Dartington Hall Trust in England and a progressive school at Dartington that explicitly invoked Rabindranath's educational ideals[5]):

> It does not need a defeatist to feel deeply anxious about the future of millions who with all their innate culture and their peaceful traditions are being simultaneously subjected to hunger, disease, exploitations foreign and indigenous, and the seething discontents of communalism.

How would Tagore have viewed the India of today, we may well ask on the fiftieth anniversary of its independence in 1947? Would he see progress there, or wasted opportunity, perhaps even a betrayal of its promise and conviction? And, on a wider subject, how would he react to the spread of cultural separatism in the contemporary world?

---

5. On Dartington Hall, the school, and the Elmhirsts, see Michael Young, *The Elmhirsts of Dartington: The Creation of an Utopian Community* (Routledge, 1982).

2

- - - - -

EAST AND WEST

GIVEN THE VAST range of his creative achievements, perhaps the most astonishing aspect of the image of Tagore in the West is its narrowness; he is recurrently viewed as "the great mystic from the East," an image with a putative message for the West, which some would welcome, others dislike, and still others find deeply boring. To a great extent this Tagore was the West's own creation, part of its tradition of message-seeking from the East, particularly from India, which—as Hegel put it—had "existed for millennia in the imagination of the Europeans."[6] Friedrich Schlegel, Schelling, Herder, and Schopenhauer were only a few of the thinkers who followed the same pattern. They theorized, at first, that India was the source of superior wisdom. Schopenhauer at one stage even argued that the New Testament "must somehow be of Indian origin: this is attested by its completely Indian ethics, which transforms morals into asceticism, its pessimism, and its avatar," in "the person of Christ." But then they rejected their own theories with great vehemence, sometimes blaming India for not living up to their unfounded expectations.

---

6. I have tried to analyze these "exotic" approaches to India (along with other Western approaches) in "India and the West," *The New Republic*, June 7, 1993, and in "Indian Traditions and the Western Imagination," *Daedalus*, Spring 1997.

We can imagine that Rabindranath's physical appearance—handsome, bearded, dressed in non-Western clothes—may, to some extent, have encouraged his being seen as a carrier of exotic wisdom. Yasunari Kawabata, the first Japanese Nobel laureate in literature, treasured memories from his middle-school days of "this sage-like poet":

64

> His white hair flowed softly down both sides of his forehead; the tufts of hair under the temples also were long like two beards, and linking up with the hair on his cheeks, continued into his beard, so that he gave an impression, to the boy I was then, of some ancient Oriental wizard.[7]

That appearance would have been well suited to the selling of Tagore in the West as a quintessentially mystical poet, and it could have made it somewhat easier to pigeonhole him. Commenting on Rabindranath's appearance, Frances Cornford told William Rothenstein, "I can now imagine a powerful and gentle Christ, which I never could before." Beatrice Webb, who did not like Tagore and resented what she took to be his "quite obvious dislike of all that the Webbs stand for" (there is, in fact, little evidence that Tagore had given much thought to this subject), said that he was "beautiful to look at" and that "his speech has the perfect intonation and slow chant-like moderation of the dramatic saint."

---

7. Yasunari Kawabata, *The Existence and Discovery of Beauty*, translated by V. H. Viglielmo (Tokyo: The Mainichi Newspapers, 1969), pp. 56–57.

Ezra Pound and W. B. Yeats, among others, first led the chorus of adoration in the Western appreciation of Tagore, and then soon moved to neglect and even shrill criticism. The contrast between Yeats's praise of his work in 1912 ("These lyrics . . . display in their thought a world I have dreamed of all my life long," "the work of a supreme culture") and his denunciation in 1935 ("Damn Tagore") arose partly from the inability of Tagore's many-sided writings to fit into the narrow box in which Yeats wanted to place—and keep—him. Certainly, Tagore did write a huge amount, and published ceaselessly, even in English (sometimes in indifferent English translation), but Yeats was also bothered, it is clear, by the difficulty of fitting Tagore's later writings into the image Yeats had presented to the West. Tagore, he had said, was the product of "a whole people, a whole civilization, immeasurably strange to us," and yet "we have met our own image, . . . or heard, perhaps for the first time in literature, our voice as in a dream."[8]

Yeats did not totally reject his early admiration (as Ezra Pound and several others did), and he included some of Tagore's early poems in *The Oxford Book of Modern Verse*, which he edited in 1936. Yeats also had some favorable things to say about Tagore's prose writings. His censure of Tagore's later poems was reinforced by his dislike of Tagore's own English translations of his work ("Tagore does not know English, no

8. W. B. Yeats, "Introduction," in Rabindranath Tagore, *Gitanjali* (London: Macmillan, 1913).

Indian knows English," Yeats explained), unlike the English version of *Gitanjali* which Yeats had himself helped to prepare. Poetry is, of course, notoriously difficult to translate, and anyone who knows Tagore's poems in their original Bengali cannot feel satisfied with any of the translations (made with or without Yeats's help). Even the translations of his prose works suffer, to some extent, from distortion. E. M. Forster noted, in a review of a translation of one of Tagore's great Bengali novels, *The Home and the World*, in 1919: "The theme is so beautiful," but the charms have "vanished in translation," or perhaps "in an experiment that has not quite come off."[9]

Tagore himself played a somewhat bemused part in the boom and bust of his English reputation. He accepted the extravagant praise with much surprise as well as pleasure, and then received denunciations with even greater surprise, and barely concealed pain. Tagore was sensitive to criticism, and was hurt by even the most far-fetched accusations, such as the charge that he was getting credit for the work of Yeats, who had "rewritten" *Gitanjali*. (This charge was made by a correspondent for *The Times*, Sir Valentine Chirol,

---

9. Tagore himself vacillated over the years about the merits of his own translations. He told his friend Sir William Rothenstein, the artist: "I am sure you remember with what reluctant hesitation I gave up to your hand my manuscript of *Gitanjali*, feeling sure that my English was of that amorphous kind for whose syntax a school-boy could be reprimanded." These—and related— issues are discussed by Nabaneeta Dev Sen, "The 'Foreign Reincarnation' of Rabindranath Tagore," *Journal of Asian Studies*, 25 (1966), reprinted, along with other relevant papers, in her *Counterpoints: Essays in Comparative Literature* (Calcutta: Prajna, 1985).

whom E. M. Forster once described as "an old Anglo-Indian reactionary hack.") From time to time Tagore also protested the crudity of some of his overexcited advocates. He wrote to C. F. Andrews in 1920: "These people . . . are like drunkards who are afraid of their lucid intervals."

3

- - - - -

GOD AND OTHERS

YEATS WAS NOT wrong to see a large religious element in Tagore's writings. He certainly had interesting and arresting things to say about life and death. Susan Owen, the mother of Wilfred Owen, wrote to Rabindranath in 1920, describing her last conversations with her son before he left for the war which would take his life. Wilfred said goodbye with "those wonderful words of yours—beginning at 'When I go from hence, let this be my parting word.'" When Wilfred's pocket notebook was returned to his mother, she found "these words written in his dear writing—with your name beneath."

The idea of a direct, joyful, and totally fearless relationship with God can be found in many of Tagore's religious writings, including the poems of *Gitanjali*. From India's diverse religious traditions he drew many ideas, both from ancient texts and from popular poetry. But "the bright pebbly eyes of the

Theosophists" do not stare out of his verses. Despite the archaic language of the original translation of *Gitanjali*, which did not, I believe, help to preserve the simplicity of the original, its elementary humanity comes through more clearly than any complex and intense spirituality:

> *Leave this chanting and singing and telling of beads!*
> *Whom dost thou worship in this lonely dark*
> *corner of a temple with doors all shut?*
> *Open thine eyes and see thy God is not before thee!*
> *He is there where the tiller is tilling the hard ground*
> *and where the pathmaker is breaking stones.*
> *He is with them in sun and in shower, and his*
> *garment is covered with dust.*

An ambiguity about religious experience is central to many of Tagore's devotional poems, and makes them appeal to readers irrespective of their beliefs; but excessively detailed interpretation can ruinously strip away that ambiguity.[10] This applies particularly to his many poems which combine images of human love and those of pious devotion. Tagore writes:

> *I have no sleep to-night. Ever and again I open my*

---

10. The importance of ambiguity and incomplete description in Tagore's poetry provides some insight into the striking thesis of William Radice (one of the major English translators of Tagore) that "his blend of poetry and prose is all the more truthful for being incomplete" ("Introduction" to his *Rabindranath Tagore: Selected Short Stories*, Penguin, 1991, p. 28).

door and look out on the darkness, my friend!
I can see nothing before me. I wonder where lies
*   thy path!*
By what dim shore of the ink-black river, by what
*   far edge of the frowning forest, through what*
*   mazy depth of gloom, art thou threading thy*
*   course to come to see me, my friend?*

I suppose it could be helpful to be told, as Yeats hastens to explain, that "the servant or the bride awaiting the master's home-coming in the empty house" is "among the images of the heart turning to God." But in Yeats's considerate attempt to make sure that the reader does not miss the "main point," something of the enigmatic beauty of the Bengali poem is lost—even what had survived the antiquated language of the English translation. Tagore certainly had strongly held religious beliefs (of an unusually nondenominational kind), but he was interested in a great many other things as well and had many different things to say about them.

Some of the ideas he tried to present were directly political, and they figure rather prominently in his letters and lectures. He had practical, plainly expressed views about nationalism, war and peace, cross-cultural education, freedom of the mind, the importance of rational criticism, the need for openness, and so on. His admirers in the West, however, were tuned to the more otherworldly themes which had been emphasized by his first Western patrons. People came to his public lectures in Europe and America, expecting ruminations on grand, transcendental themes; when they heard instead his views on the way public leaders should behave, there was some resentment, particularly (as E. P. Thompson reports) when he delivered political criticism "at $700 a scold."

4

- - - - -

REASONING IN FREEDOM

FOR TAGORE IT was of the highest importance that people be able to live, and reason, in freedom. His attitudes toward politics and culture, nationalism and internationalism, tradition and modernity, can all be seen in the light of this belief.[11] Nothing, perhaps, expresses his values as clearly as a poem in *Gitanjali*:

> *Where the mind is without fear and the head is*
> *held high;*
> *Where knowledge is free;*
> *Where the world has not been broken up into*
> *fragments by narrow domestic walls; . . . .*
> *Where the clear stream of reason has not lost its*
> *way into the dreary desert sand of dead habit; . . . .*

---

11. Satyajit Ray, the film director, has argued that even in Tagore's paintings, "the mood evoked . . . is one of a joyous freedom" (Ray, "Foreword," in Andrew Robinson, *The Art of Rabindranath Tagore*, London: André Deutsch, 1989).

*Into that heaven of freedom, my Father, let my
country awake.*

Rabindranath's qualified support for nationalist
movements—and his opposition to the unfreedom of
alien rule—came from this commitment. So did his
reservations about patriotism, which, he argued, can
limit both the freedom to engage ideas from outside
"narrow domestic walls" and the freedom also to support the causes of people in other countries. Rabindranath's passion for freedom underlies his firm
opposition to unreasoned traditionalism, which makes
one a prisoner of the past (lost, as he put it, in "the
dreary desert sand of dead habit").

Tagore illustrates the tyranny of the past in his
amusing yet deeply serious parable "Kartar Bhoot"
("The Ghost of the Leader"). As the respected leader of
an imaginary land is about to die, his panic-stricken
followers request him to stay on after his death to
instruct them on what to do. He consents. But his followers find their lives are full of rituals and constraints
on everyday behavior and are not responsive to the
world around them. Ultimately, they request the ghost
of the leader to relieve them of his domination, when
he informs them that he exists only in their minds.

Tagore's deep aversion to any commitment to the
past that could not be modified by contemporary reason extended even to the alleged virtue of invariably
keeping past promises. On one occasion when Mahatma Gandhi visited Tagore's school at Santiniketan,
a young woman got him to sign her autograph book.

Gandhi wrote: "Never make a promise in haste. Having once made it fulfill it at the cost of your life." When he saw this entry, Tagore became agitated. He wrote in the same book a short poem in Bengali to the effect that no one can be made "a prisoner forever with a chain of clay." He went on to conclude in English, possibly so that Gandhi could read it too, "Fling away your promise if it is found to be wrong."[12]

Tagore had the greatest admiration for Mahatma Gandhi as a person and as a political leader, but he was also highly skeptical of Gandhiji's form of nationalism and his conservative instincts regarding the country's past traditions. He never criticized Gandhi personally. In the 1938 essay "Gandhi the Man," he wrote:

> Great as he is as a politician, as an organizer, as a leader of men, as a moral reformer, he is greater than all these as a man, because none of these aspects and activities limits his humanity. They are rather inspired and sustained by it.

And yet there is a deep division between the two men. Tagore was explicit about his disagreement:

> We who often glorify our tendency to ignore reason, installing in its place blind faith, valuing it as spiritual, are ever paying for its cost with the obscuration of our mind and destiny. I blamed

---

12. Reported in Amita Sen, *Anando Sharbokaje* (in Bengali) (Calcutta: Tagore Research Institute, 2nd edition, 1996), p. 132.

Mahatmaji for exploiting this irrational force of credulity in our people, which might have had a quick result [in creating] a superstructure, while sapping the foundation. Thus began my estimate of Mahatmaji, as the guide of our nation, and it is fortunate for me that it did not end there.

But while it "did not end there," that difference of vision was a powerful divider.

Tagore, for example, remained unconvinced of the merit of Gandhi's forceful advocacy that everyone should spin at home with the "charka," the primitive spinning wheel. For Gandhi this practice was an important part of India's self-realization. "The spinning-wheel gradually became," as his biographer B. R. Nanda writes, "the center of rural uplift in the Gandhian scheme of Indian economics."[13] Tagore found the alleged economic rationale for this scheme quite unrealistic. As Romain Rolland noted, Rabindranath "never tires of criticizing the charka." In this economic judgment, Tagore was probably right. Except for the rather small specialized market for high-quality spun cloth, it is hard to make economic sense of hand-spinning, even with wheels less primitive than Gandhi's charka. Hand-spinning as a widespread activity can survive only with the help of heavy government subsidies.[14]

---

13. B. R. Nanda, *Mahatma Gandhi* (Oxford University Press, 1958; paperback, 1989), p. 149.

14. The economic issues are discussed in my *Choice of Techniques* (Blackwell, 1960), Appendix D.

However, Gandhi's advocacy of the charka was not based only on economics. He wanted everyone to spin for "thirty minutes every day as a sacrifice," seeing this as a way for people who are better off to identify themselves with the less fortunate. He was impatient with Tagore's refusal to grasp this point:

> The poet lives for the morrow, and would have us do likewise. . . . "Why should I, who have no need to work for food, spin?" may be the question asked. Because I am eating what does not belong to me. I am living on the spoliation of my countrymen. Trace the source of every coin that finds its way into your pocket, and you will realise the truth of what I write. Every one must spin. Let Tagore spin like the others. Let him burn his foreign clothes; that is the duty today. God will take care of the morrow.[15]

If Tagore had missed something in Gandhi's argument, so did Gandhi miss the point of Tagore's main criticism. It was not only that the charka made little economic sense, but also, Tagore thought, that it was not the way to make people reflect on anything: "The charka does not require anyone to think; one simply turns the wheel of the antiquated invention endlessly, using the minimum of judgment and stamina."

---

15. Mohandas Gandhi, quoted by Krishna Kripalani, *Tagore: A Life* (New Delhi: Orient Longman, 1961, second edition, 1971), pp. 171–172.

5

- - - - -

CELIBACY AND PERSONAL LIFE

TAGORE'S AND GANDHI'S attitudes toward personal life were also quite different. Gandhi was keen on the virtues of celibacy, theorized about it, and, after some years of conjugal life, made a private commitment—publicly announced—to refrain from sleeping with his wife. Rabindranath's own attitude on this subject was very different, but he was gentle about their disagreements:

> [Gandhiji] condemns sexual life as inconsistent with the moral progress of man, and has a horror of sex as great as that of the author of *The Kreutzer Sonata*, but, unlike Tolstoy, he betrays no abhorrence of the sex that tempts his kind. In fact, his tenderness for women is one of the noblest and most consistent traits of his character, and he counts among the women of his country some of his best and truest comrades in the great movement he is leading.

Tagore's personal life was, in many ways, an unhappy one. He married in 1883, lost his wife in 1902, and never remarried. He sought close companionship, which he did not always get (perhaps even during his married life—he wrote to his wife, Mrinalini: "If you and I could be comrades in all our work and in all our thoughts it would be splendid, but we cannot attain all that we desire"). He maintained a warm friendship with, and a strong Platonic attachment to, the literature-loving wife, Kadambari, of his elder brother, Jyotirindranath. He dedicated some poems to her before his marriage, and several books afterward, some after her death (she committed suicide, for reasons that are not fully understood, at the age of twenty-five, four months after Rabindranath's wedding).

Much later in life, during his tour of Argentina in 1924–1925, Rabindranath came to know the talented and beautiful Victoria Ocampo, who later became the publisher of the literary magazine *Sur*. They became close friends, but it appears that Rabindranath deflected the possibility of a passionate relationship into a confined intellectual one.[16] His friend Leonard Elmhirst, who accompanied Rabindranath on his Argentine tour, wrote:

> Besides having a keen intellectual understanding of his books, she was in love with him—but instead of being content to build a friendship on the basis of intellect, she was in a hurry to establish that kind of proprietary right over him which he absolutely would not brook.

16. For fuller accounts of the events, see Dutta and Robinson, *Rabindranath Tagore: The Myriad-Minded Man*, Chapter 25, and Ketaki Kushari Dyson, *In Your Blossoming Flower-Garden: Rabindranath Tagore and Victoria Ocampo* (New Delhi: Sahitya Akademi, 1988).

Ocampo and Elmhirst, while remaining friendly, were both quite rude in what they wrote about each other. Ocampo's book on Tagore (of which a Bengali translation was made from the Spanish by the distinguished poet and critic Shankha Ghosh) is primarily concerned with Tagore's writings but also discusses the pleasures and difficulties of their relationship, giving quite a different account from Elmhirst's, and never suggesting any sort of proprietary intentions.

Victoria Ocampo, however, makes it clear that she very much wanted to get physically closer to Rabindranath: "Little by little he [Tagore] partially tamed the young animal, by turns wild and docile, who did not sleep, dog-like, on the floor outside his door, simply because it was not done."[17] Rabindranath, too, was clearly very much attracted to her. He called her "Vijaya" (the Sanskrit equivalent of Victoria), dedicated a book of poems to her, *Purabi*—an "evening melody"—and expressed great admiration for her mind ("like a star that was distant"). In a letter to her he wrote, as if to explain his own reticence:

> When we were together, we mostly played with words and tried to laugh away our best opportunities to see each other clearly. . . . Whenever there is the least sign of the nest becoming a jealous

17. Published in English translation in *Rabindranath Tagore: A Centenary Volume, 1861–1961* (New Delhi: Sahitya Akademi, 1961), with an Introduction by Jawaharlal Nehru.

rival of the sky[,] my mind, like a migrant bird, tries to take . . . flight to a distant shore.

Five years later, during Tagore's European tour in 1930, he sent her a cable: "Will you not come and see me." She did. But their relationship did not seem to go much beyond conversation, and their somewhat ambiguous correspondence continued over the years. Written in 1940, a year before his death at eighty, one of the poems in *Sesh Lekha* (*Last Writings*), seems to be about her: "How I wish I could once again find my way to that foreign land where waits for me the message of love! / . . . Her language I knew not, but what her eyes said will forever remain eloquent in its anguish."[18]

However indecisive, or confused, or awkward Rabindranath may have been, he certainly did not share Mahatma Gandhi's censorious views of sex. In fact, when it came to social policy, he advocated contraception and family planning while Gandhi preferred abstinence.

---

18. English translation from Krishna Kripalani, *Tagore: A Life*, p. 185.

6

- - - - -

SCIENCE AND THE PEOPLE

GANDHI AND TAGORE severely clashed over their totally different attitudes toward science. In January 1934, Bihar was struck by a devastating earthquake which killed thousands of people. Gandhi, who was then deeply involved in the fight against untouchability (the barbaric system inherited from India's divisive past, in which "lowly people" were kept at a physical distance), extracted a positive lesson from the tragic event. "A man like me," Gandhi argued, "cannot but believe this earthquake is a divine chastisement sent by God for our sins"—in particular the sins of untouchability. "For me there is a vital connection between the Bihar calamity and the untouchability campaign."

Tagore, who equally abhorred untouchability and had joined Gandhi in the movements against it, protested against this interpretation of an event that had caused suffering and death to so many innocent people, including children and babies. He also hated the epistemology implicit in seeing an earthquake as caused by ethical failure. "It is," he wrote, "all the more unfortunate because this kind of unscientific view of [natural] phenomena is too readily accepted by a large section of our countrymen."

The two remained deeply divided over their attitudes toward science. However, while Tagore believed that modern science was essential to understanding physical phenomena, his views on epistemology were interestingly heterodox. He did not take the simple "realist" position often associated with modern science. The report of his conversation with Einstein, published in *The New York Times* in 1930, shows how insistent Tagore was on interpreting truth through observation and reflective concepts. To assert that something is true or untrue in the absence of anyone to observe or perceive its truth, or to form a conception of what it is, appeared to Tagore to be deeply questionable. When Einstein remarked, "If there were no human beings any more, the Apollo Belvedere no longer would be beautiful?" Tagore simply replied, "No." Going further—and into much more interesting territory—Einstein said, "I agree with regard to this conception of beauty, but not with regard to truth." Tagore's response was: "Why not? Truth is realized through men."[19]

Tagore's epistemology, which he never pursued systematically, would seem to be searching for a line of reasoning that would later be elegantly developed by Hilary Putnam, who has argued: "Truth depends on conceptual schemes and it is nonetheless 'real truth.'"[20] Tagore himself said little to explain his convictions, but

---

19. "Einstein and Tagore Plumb the Truth," *The New York Times Magazine*, August 10, 1930; republished in Dutta and Robinson, *Selected Letters of Rabindranath Tagore.*

20. Hilary Putnam, *The Many Faces of Realism* (Open Court, 1987). On related issues, see also Thomas Nagel, *The View from Nowhere* (Oxford University Press, 1986).

it is important to take account of his heterodoxy, not only because his speculations were invariably interest-ing, but also because they illustrate how his support for any position, including his strong interest in science, was accompanied by critical scrutiny.

7

- - - - -

NATIONALISM AND COLONIALISM

TAGORE WAS PREDICTABLY hostile to communal sectarianism (such as a Hindu orthodoxy that was antagonistic to Islamic, Christian, or Sikh per-spectives). But even nationalism seemed to him to be suspect. Isaiah Berlin summarizes well Tagore's com-plex position on Indian nationalism:

> Tagore stood fast on the narrow causeway, and did not betray his vision of the difficult truth. He condemned romantic overattachment to the past, what he called the tying of India to the past "like a sacrificial goat tethered to a post," and he accused men who displayed it—they seemed to him reactionary—of not knowing what true polit-ical freedom was, pointing out that it is from English thinkers and English books that the very notion of political liberty was derived. But against cosmopolitanism he maintained that the English stood on their own feet, and so must Indians. In

1917 he once more denounced the danger of "leaving everything to the unalterable will of the Master," be he brahmin or Englishman.[21]

The duality Berlin points to is well reflected also in Tagore's attitude toward cultural diversity. He wanted Indians to learn what is going on elsewhere, how others lived, what they valued, and so on, while remaining interested and involved in their own culture and heritage. Indeed, in his educational writings the need for synthesis is strongly stressed. It can also be found in his advice to Indian students abroad. In 1907 he wrote to his son-in-law Nagendranath Gangulee, who had gone to America to study agriculture:

> To get on familiar terms with the local people is a part of your education. To know only agriculture is not enough; you must know America too. Of course if, in the process of knowing America, one begins to lose one's identity and falls into the trap of becoming an Americanised person contemptuous of everything Indian, it is preferable to stay in a locked room.

Tagore was strongly involved in protest against the Raj on a number of occasions, most notably in the movement to resist the 1905 British proposal to split in

---

21. Isaiah Berlin, "Rabindranath Tagore and the Consciousness of Nationality," *The Sense of Reality: Studies in Ideas and Their History* (Farrar, Straus and Giroux, 1997), p. 265.

two the province of Bengal, a plan that was eventually withdrawn following popular resistance. He was forthright in denouncing the brutality of British rule in India, never more so than after the Amritsar massacre of April 13, 1919, when 379 unarmed people at a peaceful meeting were gunned down by the army, and two thousand more were wounded. Between April 23 and 26, Rabindranath wrote five agitated letters to C. F. Andrews, who himself was extremely disturbed, especially after he was told by a British civil servant in India that thanks to this show of strength, the "moral prestige" of the Raj had "never been higher."

A month after the massacre, Tagore wrote to the Viceroy of India, asking to be relieved of the knighthood he had accepted four years earlier:

> The disproportionate severity of the punishments inflicted upon the unfortunate people and the methods of carrying them out, we are convinced, are without parallel in the history of civilized governments, barring some conspicuous exceptions, recent and remote. Considering that such treatment has been meted out to a population, disarmed and resourceless, by a power which has the most terribly efficient organisation for destruction of human lives, we must strongly assert that it can claim no political expediency, far less moral justification. . . . The universal agony of indignation roused in the hearts of our people has been ignored by our rulers—possibly congratulating themselves for imparting what they imagine as

salutary lessons. . . . I for my part want to stand, shorn of all special distinctions, by the side of those of my countrymen who for their so-called insignificance are liable to suffer a degradation not fit for human beings.

Both Gandhi and Nehru expressed their appreciation of the important part Tagore took in the national struggle. It is fitting that after Independence, India chose a song of Tagore ("Jana Gana Mana Adhinayaka," which can be roughly translated as "the leader of people's minds") as its national anthem. Since Bangladesh would later choose another song of Tagore ("Amar Sonar Bangla") as its national anthem, he may be the only one ever to have authored the national anthems of two different countries.

Tagore's criticism of the British administration of India was consistently strong and grew more intense over the years. This point is often missed, since he made a special effort to dissociate his criticism of the Raj from any denigration of British—or Western—people and culture. Mahatma Gandhi's well-known quip in reply to a question, asked in England, on what he thought of Western civilization ("It would be a good idea") could not have come from Tagore's lips. He would understand the provocations to which Gandhi was responding—involving cultural conceit as well as imperial tyranny. D. H. Lawrence supplied a fine example of the former: "I become more and more surprised to see how far higher, in reality, our European civilization stands than the East, Indian and Persian, ever dreamed of. . . . This fraud of looking up to them—this wretched worship-of-Tagore attitude—is disgusting." But, unlike Gandhi, Tagore could not, even in jest, be dismissive of Western civilization.

Even in his powerful indictment of British rule in India in 1941, in a lecture which he gave on his last birthday, and which was later published as a pamphlet under the title *Crisis in Civilization*, he strains hard to maintain the distinction between opposing Western imperialism and rejecting Western civilization. While he saw India as having been "smothered under the dead weight of British administration" (adding "another great and ancient civilization for whose recent tragic history the British cannot disclaim responsibility is China"), Tagore recalls what India has gained from "discussions centred upon Shakespeare's drama and Byron's poetry and above all . . . the large-hearted liberalism of nineteenth-century English politics." The tragedy, as Tagore saw it, came from the fact that what "was truly best in their own civilization, the upholding of dignity of human relationships, has no place in the British administration of this country." "If in its place they have established, baton in hand, a reign of 'law and order,' or in other words a policeman's rule, such a mockery of civilization can claim no respect from us."

8

- - - - -

CRITIQUE OF PATRIOTISM

RABINDRANATH REBELLED AGAINST
the strongly nationalist form that the independence
movement often took, and this made him refrain from
taking a particularly active part in contemporary politics. He wanted to assert India's right to be independent
without denying the importance of what India could
learn—freely and profitably—from abroad. He was
afraid that a rejection of the West in favor of an indigenous Indian tradition was not only limiting in itself; it
could easily turn into hostility to other influences from
abroad, including Christianity, which came to parts
of India by the fourth century, Judaism, which came
through Jewish immigration shortly after the fall of
Jerusalem, as did Zoroastrianism through Parsi immigration later on (mainly in the eighth century), and, of
course—and most importantly—Islam, which has had
a very strong presence in India since the tenth century.

Tagore's criticism of patriotism is a persistent theme
in his writings. As early as 1908, he put his position
succinctly in a letter replying to the criticism of Abala
Bose, the wife of a great Indian scientist, Jagadish
Chandra Bose: "Patriotism cannot be our final spiritual
shelter; my refuge is humanity. I will not buy glass for
the price of diamonds, and I will never allow patriotism
to triumph over humanity as long as I live." His novel
Ghare Baire (*The Home and the World*) has much to

say about this theme. In the novel, Nikhil, who is keen on social reform, including women's liberation, but cool toward nationalism, gradually loses the esteem of his spirited wife, Bimala, because of his failure to be enthusiastic about anti-British agitations, which she sees as a lack of patriotic commitment. Bimala becomes fascinated with Nikhil's nationalist friend Sandip, who speaks brilliantly and acts with patriotic militancy, and she falls in love with him. Nikhil refuses to change his views: "I am willing to serve my country; but my worship I reserve for Right which is far greater than my country. To worship my country as a god is to bring a curse upon it."[22]

As the story unfolds, Sandip becomes angry with some of his countrymen for their failure to join the struggle as readily as he thinks they should ("Some Mohamedan traders are still obdurate"). He arranges to deal with the recalcitrants by burning their meager trading stocks and physically attacking them. Bimala has to acknowledge the connection between Sandip's rousing nationalistic sentiments and his sectarian—and ultimately violent—actions. The dramatic events that follow (Nikhil attempts to help the victims, risking his life) include the end of Bimala's political romance.

This is a difficult subject, and Satyajit Ray's beautiful film of *The Home and the World* brilliantly brings

---

22. Martha Nussbaum initiates her wide-ranging critique of patriotism (in a debate that is joined by many others) by quoting this passage from *The Home and the World* (in Martha C. Nussbaum et al., *For Love of Country*, edited by Joshua Cohen, Beacon Press, 1996, pp. 3–4).

out the novel's tensions, along with the human affec-
tions and disaffections of the story. Not surprisingly,
the story has had many detractors, not just among dedicated nationalists in India. Georg Lukács found
Tagore's novel to be "a petit bourgeois yarn of the
shoddiest kind," "at the intellectual service of the British
police," and "a contemptible caricature of Gandhi." It
would, of course, be absurd to think of Sandip as
Gandhi, but the novel gives a "strong and gentle"
warning, as Bertolt Brecht noted in his diary, of the
corruptibility of nationalism, since it is not even-
handed. Hatred of one group can lead to hatred of
others, no matter how far such feeling may be from
the minds of large-hearted nationalist leaders like
Mahatma Gandhi.

9

- - - - -

ADMIRATION AND
CRITICISM OF JAPAN

TAGORE'S REACTION TO nationalism in
Japan is particularly telling. As in the case of India,
he saw the need to build the self-confidence of a
defeated and humiliated people, of people left behind
by developments elsewhere, as was the case in Japan
before its emergence during the nineteenth century. At
the beginning of one of his lectures in Japan in 1916
("Nationalism in Japan"), he observed that "the worst

form of bondage is the bondage of dejection, which keeps men hopelessly chained in loss of faith in themselves." Tagore shared the admiration for Japan widespread in Asia for demonstrating the ability of an Asian nation to rival the West in industrial development and economic progress. He noted with great satisfaction that Japan had "in giant strides left centuries of inaction behind, overtaking the present time in its foremost achievement." For other nations outside the West, he said, Japan "has broken the spell under which we lay in torpor for ages, taking it to be the normal condition of certain races living in certain geographical limits."

But then Tagore went on to criticize the rise of a strong nationalism in Japan, and its emergence as an imperialist nation. Tagore's outspoken criticisms did not please Japanese audiences and, as E. P. Thompson wrote, "the welcome given to him on his first arrival soon cooled."[23] Twenty-two years later, in 1937, during the Japanese war on China, Tagore received a letter from Rash Behari Bose, an anti-British Indian revolutionary then living in Japan, who sought Tagore's approval for his efforts there on behalf of Indian independence, in which he had the support of the Japanese government. Tagore replied:

> Your cable has caused me many restless hours, for it hurts me very much to have to ignore your appeal. I wish you had asked for my cooperation

---

23. E. P. Thompson, Introduction to Tagore's *Nationalism* (London, Macmillan, 1991), p. 10.

in a cause against which my spirit did not protest. I know, in making this appeal, you counted on my great regard for the Japanese for I, along with the rest of Asia, did once admire and look up to Japan and did once fondly hope that in Japan Asia had at last discovered its challenge to the West, that Japan's new strength would be consecrated in safeguarding the culture of the East against alien interests. But Japan has not taken long to betray that rising hope and repudiate all that seemed significant in her wonderful, and, to us symbolic, awakening, and has now become itself a worse menace to the defenceless peoples of the East.

How to view Japan's position in the Second World War was a divisive issue in India. After the war, when Japanese political leaders were tried for war crimes, the sole dissenting voice among the judges came from the Indian judge, Radhabinod Pal, a distinguished jurist. Pal dissented on various grounds, among them that no fair trial was possible in view of the asymmetry of power between the victor and the defeated. Ambivalent feelings in India toward the Japanese military aggression, given the unacceptable nature of British imperialism, possibly had a part in predisposing Pal to consider a perspective different from that of the other judges.

More tellingly, Subhas Chandra Bose (no relation of Rash Behari Bose), a leading nationalist, made his way to Japan during the war via Italy and Germany after escaping from a British prison; he helped the Japanese

to form units of Indian soldiers, who had earlier sur-
rendered to the advancing Japanese army, to fight on
the Japanese side as the "Indian National Army."
Rabindranath had formerly entertained great admiration for Subhas Bose as a dedicated nonsectarian fighter
for Indian independence.[24] But their ways would have
parted when Bose's political activities took this turn,
although Tagore was dead by the time Bose reached
Japan.

Tagore saw Japanese militarism as illustrating the
way nationalism can mislead even a nation of great
achievement and promise. In 1938 Yone Noguchi, the
distinguished poet and friend of Tagore (as well as of
Yeats and Pound), wrote to Tagore, pleading with
him to change his mind about Japan. Rabindranath's
reply, written on September 12, 1938, was altogether
uncompromising:

> It seems to me that it is futile for either of us to try
> to convince the other, since your faith in the infal-
> lible right of Japan to bully other Asiatic nations
> into line with your Government's policy is not
> shared by me.... Believe me, it is sorrow and
> shame, not anger, that prompt me to write to you.
> I suffer intensely not only because the reports of
> Chinese suffering batter against my heart, but

---

24. For a lucid and informative analysis of the role of Subhas Chandra Bose
and his brother Sarat in Indian politics, see Leonard A. Gordon, *Brothers
against the Raj: A Biography of Indian Nationalists Sarat and Subhas
Chandra Bose* (Columbia University Press, 1990).

because I can no longer point out with pride the example of a great Japan.

He would have been much happier with the postwar emergence of Japan as a peaceful power. Then, too, since he was not free of egotism, he would also have been pleased by the attention paid to his ideas by the novelist Yasunari Kawabata and others.[25]

10

INTERNATIONAL CONCERNS

TAGORE WAS NOT invariably well-informed about international politics. He allowed himself to be entertained by Mussolini in a short visit to Italy in May–June 1926, a visit arranged by Carlo Formichi, professor of Sanskrit at the University of Rome. When he asked to meet Benedetto Croce, Formichi said, "Impossible! Impossible!" Mussolini told him that Croce was "not in Rome." When Tagore said he would go "wherever he is," Mussolini assured him that Croce's whereabouts were unknown.

Such incidents, as well as warnings from Romain

---

25. Kawabata made considerable use of Tagore's ideas, and even built on Tagore's thesis that it "is easier for a stranger to know what it is in [Japan] which is truly valuable for all mankind" (*The Existence and Discovery of Beauty*, pp. 55–58).

Rolland and other friends, should have ended Tagore's flirtation with Mussolini more quickly than they did. But only after he received graphic accounts of the brutality of Italian fascism from two exiles, Gaetano Salvemini and Gaetano Salvadori, and learned more of what was happening in Italy, did he publicly denounce the regime, publishing a letter to the *Manchester Guardian* in August. The next month, *Popolo d'Italia*, the magazine edited by Benito Mussolini's brother, replied: "Who cares? Italy laughs at Tagore and those who brought this unctuous and insupportable fellow in our midst."

With his high expectations of Britain, Tagore continued to be surprised by what he took to be a lack of official sympathy for international victims of aggression. He returned to this theme in the lecture he gave on his last birthday, in 1941:

> While Japan was quietly devouring North China, her act of wanton aggression was ignored as a minor incident by the veterans of British diplomacy. We have also witnessed from this distance how actively the British statesmen acquiesced in the destruction of the Spanish Republic.

But distinguishing between the British government and the British people, Rabindranath went on to note "with admiration how a band of valiant Englishmen laid down their lives for Spain."

Tagore's view of the Soviet Union has been a subject of much discussion. He was widely read in Russia. In 1917 several Russian translations of *Gitanjali* (one edited by Ivan Bunin, later the first Russian Nobel laureate in literature) were available, and by the late 1920s many of the English versions of his work had been rendered into Russian by several distinguished translators. Russian versions of his work continued to appear: Boris Pasternak translated him in the 1950s and 1960s.

When Tagore visited Russia in 1930, he was much impressed by its development efforts and by what he saw as a real commitment to eliminate poverty and economic inequality. But what impressed him most was the expansion of basic education across the old Russian empire. In *Letters from Russia*, written in Bengali and published in 1931, he unfavorably compares the acceptance of widespread illiteracy in India by the British administration with Russian efforts to expand education:

> In stepping on the soil of Russia, the first thing that caught my eye was that in education, at any rate, the peasant and the working classes have made such enormous progress in these few years that nothing comparable has happened even to our highest classes in the course of the last hundred and fifty years. . . . The people here are not at all afraid of giving complete education even to Turcomans of distant Asia; on the contrary, they are utterly in earnest about it.[26]

26. Tagore, *Letters from Russia*, translated from Bengali by Sasadhar Sinha (Calcutta: Visva-Bharati, 1960), p. 108.

When parts of the book were translated into English in 1934, the undersecretary for India stated in Parliament that it was "calculated by distortion of the facts to bring the British Administration in India into contempt and disrepute," and the book was then promptly banned. The English version would not be published until after Independence.

11

- - - - -

EDUCATION AND FREEDOM

THE BRITISH INDIAN administrators were not, however, alone in trying to suppress Tagore's reflections on Russia. They were joined by Soviet officials. In an interview with *Izvestia* in 1930, Tagore sharply criticized the lack of freedom that he observed in Russia:

> I must ask you: Are you doing your ideal a service by arousing in the minds of those under your training anger, class-hatred, and revengefulness against those whom you consider to be your enemies? . . . Freedom of mind is needed for the reception of truth; terror hopelessly kills it. . . . For the sake of humanity I hope you may never create a vicious force of violence, which will go on weaving an interminable chain of violence and cruelty. . . . You have tried to destroy many of the

other evils of [the tsarist] period. Why not try to destroy this one also?

The interview was not published in *Izvestia* until 1988—nearly sixty years later.[27]

Tagore's reaction to the Russia of 1930 arose from two of his strongest commitments: his uncompromising belief in the importance of "freedom of mind" (the source of his criticism of the Soviet Union), and his conviction that the expansion of basic education is central to social progress (the source of his praise, particularly in contrast to British-run India). He identified the lack of basic education as the fundamental cause of many of India's social and economic afflictions:

> In my view the imposing tower of misery which today rests on the heart of India has its sole foundation in the absence of education. Caste divisions, religious conflicts, aversion to work, precarious economic conditions—all centre on this single factor.

It was on education (and on the reflection, dialogue, and communication that are associated with it), rather than on, say, spinning "as a sacrifice" ("the charka does not require anyone to think"), that the future of India would depend.

---

27. It was, however, published in the *Manchester Guardian* shortly after it was meant to be published in *Izvestia*. On this see Dutta and Robinson, *Rabindranath Tagore: The Myriad-Minded Man*, p. 297.

Tagore was concerned not only that there be wider opportunities for education across the country (especially in rural areas where schools were few), but also that the schools themselves be more lively and enjoyable. He himself had dropped out of school early, largely out of boredom, and had never bothered to earn a diploma. He wrote extensively on how schools should be made more attractive to boys and girls and thus more productive. His own coeducational school at Santiniketan had many progressive features. The emphasis here was on self-motivation rather than on discipline, and on fostering intellectual curiosity rather than competitive excellence.

Much of Rabindranath's life was spent in developing the school at Santiniketan. The school never had much money, since the fees were very low. His lecture honoraria, "$700 a scold," went to support it, as well as most of his Nobel Prize money. The school received no support from the government, but did get help from private citizens—even Mahatma Gandhi raised money for it.

The dispute with Mahatma Gandhi on the Bihar earthquake touched on a subject that was very important to Tagore: the need for education in science as well as in literature and the humanities. At Santiniketan, there were strong "local" elements in its emphasis on Indian traditions, including the classics, and in the use of Bengali rather than English as the language of instruction. At the same time there were courses on a great variety of cultures, and study programs devoted to China, Japan, and the Middle East. Many foreigners came to Santiniketan to study or teach, and the fusion of studies seemed to work.

I am partial to seeing Tagore as an educator, having myself been educated at Santiniketan. The school was unusual in many different ways, such as the oddity that classes, excepting those requiring a laboratory, were held outdoors (whenever the weather permitted). No matter what we thought of Rabindranath's belief that one gains from being in a natural setting while learning (some of us argued about this theory), we typically found the experience of outdoor schooling extremely attractive and pleasant. Academically, our school was not particularly exacting (often we did not have any examinations at all), and it could not, by the usual academic standards, compete with some of the better schools in Calcutta. But there was something remarkable about the ease with which class discussions could move from Indian traditional literature to contemporary as well as classical Western thought, and then to the culture of China or Japan or elsewhere. The school's celebration of variety was also in sharp contrast with the cultural conservatism and separatism that has tended to grip India from time to time.

The cultural give and take of Tagore's vision of the contemporary world has close parallels with the vision of Satyajit Ray, also an alumnus of Santiniketan who made several films based on Tagore's stories.[28] Ray's

---

28. Satyajit Ray, *Our Films Their Films* (Calcutta: Disha Book/Orient Longman, third edition, 1993). I have tried to discuss these issues in my Satyajit Ray Memorial Lecture, "Our Culture, Their Culture," *The New Republic*, April 1, 1996.

words about Santiniketan in 1991 would have greatly
pleased Rabindranath:

> I consider the three years I spent in Santiniketan
> as the most fruitful of my life.... Santiniketan
> opened my eyes for the first time to the splen-
> dours of Indian and Far Eastern art. Until then I
> was completely under the sway of Western art,
> music and literature. Santiniketan made me the
> combined product of East and West that I am.[29]

12

- - - -

FIFTY YEARS
AFTER INDEPENDENCE

AS THE FIFTIETH anniversary of Indian independence approaches, the reckoning of what India has
or has not achieved in this half-century is becoming a
subject of considerable interest: "What has been the
story of those first fifty years?" (as Shashi Tharoor asks
in his balanced, informative, and highly readable
account of *India: From Midnight to the Millennium*).[30]
If Tagore were to see the India of today, half a century
after Independence, nothing perhaps would shock him
so much as the continued illiteracy of the masses. He

---

29. *The Guardian*, August 1, 1991.

30. Arcade Publishing, 1997, p. 1.

would see this as a total betrayal of what the nationalist leaders had promised during the struggle for independence—a promise that had figured even in Nehru's
rousing speech on the eve of Independence in August
1947 (on India's "tryst with destiny").

In view of his interest in childhood education,
Tagore would not be consoled by the extraordinary
expansion of university education, in which India
sends to its universities six times as many people per
unit of population as does China. Rather, he would be
stunned that, in contrast to East and Southeast Asia,
including China, half the adult population and two
thirds of Indian women remain unable to read or write.
Statistically reliable surveys indicate that even in the
late 1980s, nearly half of the rural girls between the
ages of twelve and fourteen did not attend any school
for a single day of their lives.[31]

This state of affairs is the result of the continuation of British imperial neglect of mass education,
which has been reinforced by India's traditional
elitism, as well as upper-class–dominated contemporary politics (except in parts of India such as Kerala,
where anti–upper-caste movements have tended to
concentrate on education as a great leveler). Tagore
would see illiteracy and the neglect of education
not only as the main source of India's continued

31. On this and related issues, see Jean Drèze and Amartya Sen, *India:
Economic Development and Social Opportunity* (Clarendon Press/Oxford
University Press, 1996), particularly Chapter 6, and also Drèze and Sen, edi-
tors, *Indian Development: Selected Regional Perspectives* (Clarendon
Press/Oxford University Press, 1996).

social backwardness, but also as a great constraint that restricts the possibility and reach of economic development in India (as his writings on rural development forcefully make clear). Tagore would also have strongly felt the need for a greater commitment— and a greater sense of urgency—in removing endemic poverty.

At the same time, Tagore would undoubtedly find some satisfaction in the survival of democracy in India, in its relatively free press, and in general from the "freedom of mind" that post-Independence Indian politics has, on the whole, managed to maintain. He would also be pleased by the fact noted by the historian E. P. Thompson (whose father, Edward Thompson, had written one of the first major biographies of Tagore[32]):

> All the convergent influences of the world run through this society: Hindu, Moslem, Christian, secular; Stalinist, liberal, Maoist, democratic socialist, Gandhian. There is not a thought that is being thought in the West or East that is not active in some Indian mind.[33]

Tagore would have been happy also to see that the one governmental attempt to dispense generally with basic liberties and political and civil rights in India, in the 1970s, when Prime Minister Indira Gandhi (ironically,

---

32. Edward Thompson, *Rabindranath Tagore: Poet and Dramatist* (Oxford University Press, 1926).

33. Quoted in Shashi Tharoor, *India*, p. 9.

herself a former student at Santiniketan) declared an "emergency," was overwhelmingly rejected by the Indian voters, leading to the precipitate fall of her government.

Rabindranath would also see that the changes in policy that have eliminated famine since Independence had much to do with the freedom to be heard in a democratic India. In Tagore's play *Raja O Rani* ("The King and the Queen"), the sympathetic Queen eventually rebels against the callousness of state policy toward the hungry. She begins by inquiring about the ugly sounds outside the palace, only to be told that the noise is coming from "the coarse, clamorous crowd who howl unashamedly for food and disturb the sweet peace of the palace." The Viceregal office in India could have taken a similarly callous view of Indian famines, right up to the easily preventable Bengal famine of 1943, just before Independence, which killed between two and three million people. But a government in a multi-party democracy, with elections and free newspapers, cannot any longer dismiss the noise from "the coarse, clamorous crowd."[34]

Unlike Gandhiji, Rabindranath would not resent the development of modern industries in India, or the acceleration of technical progress, since he did not

---

34. I have tried to discuss the linkage between democracy, political incentives, and prevention of disasters in *Resources, Values and Development* (Harvard University Press, 1984, reprinted 1997), Chapter 19, and in my presidential address to the American Economic Association, "Rationality and Social Choice," *American Economic Review*, 85 (1995).

want India to be shackled to the turning of "the wheel of an antiquated invention." Tagore was concerned that people not be dominated by machines, but he was not opposed to making good use of modern technology. "The mastery over the machine," he wrote in *Crisis in Civilization*, "by which the British have consolidated their sovereignty over their vast empire, has been kept a sealed book, to which due access has been denied to this helpless country." Rabindranath had a deep interest in the environment—he was particularly concerned about deforestation and initiated a "festival of tree-planting" (*vriksha-ropana*) as early as 1928. He would want increased private and government commitments to environmentalism; but he would not derive from this position a general case against modern industry and technology.

13

- - - - -

ON CULTURAL SEPARATISM

RABINDRANATH WOULD BE shocked by the growth of cultural separatism in India, as elsewhere. The "openness" that he valued so much is certainly under great strain right now—in many countries. Religious fundamentalism still has a relatively small following in India; but various factions seem to be doing their best to increase their numbers. Certainly religious sectarianism has had much success in some parts of India (particularly in the west and the north). Tagore would see the expansion of religious sectarianism as being closely associated with an artificially separatist view of culture.

He would have strongly resisted defining India in specifically Hindu terms, rather than as a "confluence" of many cultures. Even after the Partition of 1947, India is still the third-largest Muslim country in the world, with more Muslims than in Bangladesh, and nearly as many as in Pakistan. Only Indonesia has substantially more followers of Islam. Indeed, by pointing to the immense heterogeneousness of India's cultural background and its richly diverse history, Tagore had argued that the "idea of India" itself militated against a culturally separatist view—"against the intense consciousness of the separateness of one's own people from others."

Tagore would also oppose the cultural nationalism that has recently been gaining some ground in India, along with an exaggerated fear of the influence of the West. He was uncompromising in his belief that human beings could absorb quite different cultures in constructive ways:

> Whatever we understand and enjoy in human products instantly becomes ours, wherever they might have their origin. I am proud of my humanity when I can acknowledge the poets and artists of other countries as my own. Let me feel with unalloyed gladness that all the great glories of man are mine. Therefore it hurts me deeply when

the cry of rejection rings loud against the West in
my country with the clamour that Western education can only injure us.

In this context, it is important to emphasize that
Rabindranath was not short of pride in India's own
heritage, and often spoke about it. He lectured at
Oxford, with evident satisfaction, on the importance of
India's religious ideas—quoting both from ancient
texts and from popular poetry (such as the verses of
the sixteenth-century Muslim poet Kabir). In 1940,
when he was given an honorary doctorate by Oxford
University, in a ceremony arranged at his own educational establishment in Santiniketan ("In Gangem
Defluit Isis," Oxford helpfully explained), to the pre-
dictable "volley of Latin" Tagore responded "by a volley of Sanskrit," as Marjorie Sykes, a Quaker friend of
Rabindranath, reports. Her cheerful summary of the
match, "India held its own," was not out of line with
Tagore's pride in Indian culture. His welcoming attitude to Western civilization was reinforced by this confidence: he did not see India's culture as fragile and in
need of "protection" from Western influence.

In India, he wrote, "circumstances almost compel us
to learn English, and this lucky accident has given us
the opportunity of access into the richest of all poetical
literatures of the world." There seems to me much
force in Rabindranath's argument for clearly distinguishing between the injustice of a serious asymmetry
of power (colonialism being a prime example of this)
and the importance nevertheless of appraising Western

culture in an open-minded way, in colonial and post-colonial territories, in order to see what uses could be made of it.

Rabindranath insisted on open debate on every issue, and distrusted conclusions based on a mechanical formula, no matter how attractive that formula might seem in isolation (such as "This was forced on us by our colonial masters—we must reject it," "This is our tradition—we must follow it," "We have promised to do this—we must fulfill that promise," and so on). The question he persistently asks is whether we have reason enough to want what is being proposed, taking everything into account. Important as history is, reasoning has to go beyond the past. It is in the sovereignty of reasoning—fearless reasoning in freedom—that we can find Rabindranath Tagore's lasting voice.[35]

35. For helpful discussions I am most grateful to Akeel Bilgrami, Sissela Bok, Sugata Bose, Supratik Bose, Krishna Dutta, Rounaq Jahan, Salim Jahan, Marufi Khan, Andrew Robinson, Nandana Sen, Gayatri Chakravorty Spivak, and Shashi Tharoor.

Anita
Desai

- - - - -

"Women
Well Set
Free"

IN 1910, BANGALORE Nagaratnamma, described as "a patron of the arts, a learned woman, a musician, and a distinguished courtesan," decided to reprint the Telugu classic *Radhika Santwanam* (*Appeasing Radhika*) by the eighteenth-century poet Muddupalani "not only [because it was] written by a woman, but by one who was born into our community," and because she found it "as adorable as the young Lord Krishna." She added, in her afterword, "However often I read this book, I feel like reading it all over again."

The author of the epic poem was an equally unusual woman (unusual to us and not, it seems, in her own time). Her autobiographical prologue—a convention of such work—reveals that she was a celebrated courtesan of the Thanjavur court in the reign of Pratapasimha (1739–1763), a poet who traced her lineage through her aunt and grandmother, and an accomplished dancer and musician. She writes of her beauty and learning and her status among other poets and scholars of the court with a straightforwardness and lack of coyness that indicate both confidence and security:

Which other woman of my kind has
felicitated scholars with gifts and money?
To which other women of my kind have
* epics been dedicated?*
Which other woman of my kind has
won such acclaim in each of the arts?
You are incomparable,
Muddupalani, among your kind.

Nevertheless, Nagaratnamma—who had first found a reference to Muddupalani in a commentary on Thanjavur literature—had trouble in locating a copy of *Radhika Santwanam* and, when she did, found only a poorly printed version brought out in 1897 with many omissions and excisions. She managed to obtain the original manuscript and prepared a new version that was published by a small press which specialized in Telugu and Sanskrit classics. She had the misfortune of doing so in an age no longer receptive to such poetry. A leader of the social reform movement of the day denounced Muddupalani as "an adulteress. Many parts of the book are such that they should never be heard by a woman, let alone emerge from a woman's mouth." Since she was "born into a community of prostitutes and does not have the modesty natural to women," she had filled her poem with "crude descriptions of sex." Nagaratnamma defended the work stoutly:

If that is so, it should be just as wrong for men who are considered respectable to write in that manner. But, [as everyone knows] several great men have written even more "crudely" about sex.

The excerpts from Muddupalani's epic poem produced in *Women Writing in India*,[1] the anthology edited by Susie Tharu and K. Lalita, are brief but justify their claim that she brought the rhythms of classical Telugu verse closer to the spoken form, and that she celebrated a young girl's coming-of-age and her experience of sex with an unexpected and sophisticated twist. Erotic poetry in India is traditionally cast in the form of the Lord Krishna wooing the milkmaid Radha; but in *Radhika Santwanam* it is she who takes the initiative and it is her satisfaction that is central. One finds oneself amazed that such a radical interpretation was accepted in her day.

In 1910 it was not. Queen Victoria was not only the Queen of England but the Empress of India and left her mark upon the Indian scene, which was, in the eyes of her administrators, a debauched, perverse, and horrifying one. Police Officer Cunningham seized all copies of *Radhika Santwanam* and charged the publishers with producing an obscene book. Although a petition was made and scholars and lawyers argued that such proceedings were "highly detrimental to the preservation and progress of Telugu culture" and pleaded that the case should be heard by a judge who knew Telugu, Nagaratnamma and the publishers lost the case. It was only in 1947, when India had won independence, that an influential chief minister who was a nationalist had the ban withdrawn, and in 1952 a new edition was brought out.

1. *Vol. I: 600 BC to the Early Twentieth Century* (The Feminist Press at the City University of New York, 1991).

However, when the editors of this anthology searched for a copy, it proved hard to find. It is a testimony to their dedication and assiduity that it is included here along with other writing by women that they have collected in order that it might

> illuminate the condition in which women wrote; bring more significant women's writing to light; help us reevaluate writers who were reasonably well known but had been dismissed or misunderstood; give us a sense of the themes and literary modes women drew on and made use of; and help us capture that which is at stake in the practices of self or agency and of narrative that emerge at the contested margins of patriarchy, empire, and nation.

Muddupalani was only one of these writers but her story reads like an allegory of their intentions and achievements. Moreover, the publishing history of Muddupalani's work covers the historical span of the two collections under review[2] in that it moves from a precolonial, traditional age through one of social reform and nationalism to that of independence. Nagaratnamma could well be named the patron saint of the efforts of the editors of these anthologies; they have inherited her diligence, her dedication, and her values.

---

2. Tharu and Lalita, *Women Writing in India*; *Truth Tales: Contemporary Stories by Women Writers of India* edited by Kali for Women (The Feminist Press at the City University of New York, 1990).

Muddupalani did not belong to the pre-Vedic age (the time before Hinduism was made a formal system by the act of composing its scriptures in the official language, Sanskrit), but can be said to celebrate its values in art—the values of a rural, agricultural, and tribal society that inhabited India before the Aryans began their invasion in 1700 BC, characterized by *Loka-yata*—"that which is essentially this-worldly," a materialist way of thought to which *Prakriti*, the female principle, was fundamental. The deities of the time were female, the religion fertility worship.

The collection of women's folk songs presented here can be said to represent their largely oral tradition. Sung in celebration of the cycle of the agricultural year, they are set to the rhythm of agricultural tasks like threshing, winnowing, husking, spinning and weaving, and rocking the cradle. There are also songs that accompany wedding ceremonies—generally bawdy—as well as poignant songs of a bride's leavetaking of her parents and pining for home:

O Boatman, brother from the upstream country.

When you meet my father tell him about me. I watch
The boats come and go. So many of them!

If my brother doesn't hasten to take me home,
Tell him he should bring a bamboo bier to carry
    me to the grave.
Tell my mother, O brother boatman, about me,
I throw myself at your feet.

The songs composed by the Buddhist nuns in the sixth century BC and written down around 80 BC belong to what was probably the earliest anthology of women's literature in the world, the *Therigatha*. Buddhism was created as an ideology to counter the authority of the Brahmins and the sacrificial rituals of the Vedas, and represents a rebellion against patriarchy that the nuns expressed as the release of the human soul from worldly suffering in earthy metaphors easily recognizable even today:

> *A woman well set free! How free I am,*
> *How wonderfully free, from kitchen drudgery.*
> *Free from the harsh grip of hunger*
> *And from the empty cooking pots,*
> *Free too of that unscrupulous man,*
> *The weaver of sunshades.*
> *Calm now, and serene I am,*
> *All lust and hatred purged.*
> *To the shade of the spreading tree I go*
> *And contemplate my happiness.*

> "SUMANGALAMATA"

As for secular literature, Sangam poetry in Tamil of 100 BC–250 AD also gives us a great deal of textual evidence that it belonged to a pre-Aryan society. It has no references to Vedic gods and celebrates an agricultural economy—forests, pastures, well-watered valleys, and verdant mountain slopes, where cattle are the index of wealth and warriors who protect the settlements are

extolled for their valor in battle. If there is a philosophy, it is animist: no transcendent or divine being is
worshiped, but the spirit immanent in things. Chiefly it
is love and the rites of courtship that are celebrated in
the poems, with a fresh and vivid imagery drawn from
the forests and fields, with that intricate and subtle
interweaving of the religious and philosophical with
the earthly and erotic that characterizes so much Indian
art. The poetry of Akkamahadevi best represents the
intimacy of the relationship of the human with the
divine, while the prostitute-poet Sankavva juxtaposes
the sacred with the profane with startling effect. She
promises the god Shiva to give herself to no one but him:

> *In my harlot's trade*
> *having taken one man's money*
> *I daren't take a second man's, sir....*
>
> *Ah, never, no.*
>   *Knowing you I will not.*
> *My word on it,*
>   *libertine Shiva.*

"IN MY HARLOT'S TRADE"

Although two hymns in the *Rig Veda*, the oldest and
largest of the Hindu Vedas, are attributed to women,
there is no other literature by women of the Vedic
period—probably because women were not permitted
access to Sanskrit, which was the preserve of men of
the Brahmin caste only. No wonder, then, that the

Aryan woman remains a shadow of the Aryan man, subservient, dutiful, and loyal, embodying male ideals of womanhood. Yet it is a period that must be studied since "ancient India" is generally regarded as Vedic India, and such studies were in fact undertaken by officials of the East India Company who needed a knowledge of the history, legal practices, and customs of the people they had set out to govern. William Jones (1746–1794) undertook the project and extended it into the study of Sanskrit. The leading Orientalist Friedrich Max Müller (1832–1900) thought that

> so deeply have the religious and moral ideas of that primitive era taken root in the mind of the Indian nation, so minutely has almost every private and public act of Indian life been regulated by old traditionary precepts, that it is impossible to find the right point of view for judging Indian religion, morals and literature without a knowledge of the literary remains of the Vedic age.

Since these "remains" contain little or nothing by women, one might think the editors could overlook this particular period, but actually it is of vital importance to women's issues, since Vedic society was a patriarchal society and, by eulogizing it as a utopia of the Romantic imagination, both Indologists and the nationalists, who naturally preferred their benign vision to the harshly critical one of British officialdom and evangelical missionaries, endorsed the system and saw to its continuation.

Because such people "obscured and subordinated other schemes and narratives," the editors have performed a valuable service in resurrecting these pre-Aryan and non-Aryan texts, sacred and secular, which belonged to the indigenous, non-Vedic culture of India. Of course a good deal of natural assimilation later took place—e.g., the male gods of the Vedas acquired "wives," the goddesses of the Hindu pantheon, and the favorite Lord Krishna was no fair Aryan but a dark indigene, and the female form continued to be a potent icon of fertility.

One has to wait, nevertheless, until the eighth century before one sees any more poetry composed by women, and then it was the bhakti (devotional) songs composed all over India in many of the regional languages—Bengali, Marathi, Gujarati, Hindi, and Telugu being represented here. Bhakti was a protest movement against the patriarchy of Brahminic Hinduism, against pedantry and ascetic withdrawal, eulogizing instead the intensely subjective nature of mystical union with the divine. It was a people's revolt against the upper castes and the rituals performed by Brahmin priests. It required no institutional place, it could be sung in a temple, court, house, or field, composed in any language, its imagery drawn from everyday life.

The appeal it had to women is obvious. Those who chafed against the limitations of family and home broke away and wandered freely, singing the songs into which they wove their names, for these were not recorded until two centuries later. A religious rather than a political movement, it was said to "destroy the stupor that prevailed in the hearts of women and sudras . . . and brought into their lives an activating faith," but by the seventeenth century it became reduced to cults around Vedic gods and was absorbed into the temple rituals of the central system it had initially opposed. Even rebels like Mirabai (c. 1498–1565), who had scandalized society by abandoning her royal husband and home for the life of a wandering poet-singer on the pilgrim routes of India, became recast in the popular imagination to conform to respectable norms: a devotee of Krishna, she was depicted as his dutiful wife.

By the seventeenth century secular literature came to the forefront, and the accounts we have of the kingdoms of the medieval age, especially of the Moghuls, depict a society that gloried in painting, music, architecture, textiles, and poetry. Women are generally thought to have led confined lives in purdah but certainly the ladies of the courts were often highly educated and accomplished, and among them were powerful queens and consorts. Gul-Badan (1523–1603), the sister of the emperor Humayun, wrote an account of his reign that charms with its fascinating detail about the daily life of the court. In the excerpt chosen here, we have an astonishing account of the young girl Hamida, later the emperor's wife, repeatedly refusing his offer of marriage and showing an extreme reluctance to accept one from a man so much older, "an opium eater and already much married." When her mother argues, "After all, you will marry someone. Better than a king, who is there?" Hamida replies: "Oh yes, I shall marry someone; but he shall be a man whose collar my hand can touch, and not one whose skirt it does not reach." Another patron saint for this anthology, surely!

Apart from the royal and privileged, there were other women who found in the courts rich patrons of their arts. Among them was Muddupalani of the Thanjavur court of the south, and in the north there were the *tawaifs*, or courtesans, often learned, accomplished women held in high regard, sought after and wealthy, able to endow caravanserais and public gardens and monuments, as well as own and run estates.

Such women suffered along with others when the British established economic, military, and administrative rule in India. The native rulers had to pay taxes to the British and could no longer support a retinue of artists and scholars, who fell upon bad times and were reduced to penury and prostitution. The Indian peasantry suffered under new laws of taxation that were ferociously enforced even when crops failed, and the new tariffs made certain that Britain's industrial revolution thrived, while Indian workers were out of work. Famines swept the country, and women found themselves losing their traditional jobs of sowing and transplanting, winnowing and husking, as well as spinning and weaving. Peasant revolts broke out everywhere and even an official of the East India Company lamented, in 1709, "This fine country which flourished under the most despotic and arbitrary government is verging towards ruin." Yet this period of great oppression and struggle came to be known, through the efforts of British administrators and evangelical missionaries, as one of "progress" and "reform," the reform marking changes in the family structure and system, not in the relationship of the economic classes as in the West.

Certainly much of the reform was necessary and beneficial to women—*sati* (the practice of burning widows on their husbands' funeral pyres) was made illegal in 1829, widow remarriage legalized in 1856, women's education given its first impetus in 1860, while in the 1880s and 1890s child marriage was discouraged. The editors however assert that these practices actually affected small groups of women and were not known among the poor (not quite borne out by the texts in which the ill treatment of widows and child wives is taken up by writer after writer), and that the creation of the new respectable middle class had the effect of delegitimizing and marginalizing many artists.

Bhakti singers who had once been welcomed into upper-class homes for their music and as teachers to their children now became unacceptable in "respectable" homes. Popular culture was discredited, and the sexuality of middle-class women contained. The census figures bear out the thesis of the editors startlingly: in 1891 there were 17,023 actresses, in 1901 only 3,527. One of them was Binodini Dasi, who, in *My Story*, claims that she took on the responsibility of raising money to build a theater in Calcutta and was encouraged by her male colleagues to live with rich men for their presents, only to find that instead of naming it after her as she had expected, they called it the Star

Theater and edged her out as soon as her mission was accomplished. Lalithambika Antherjanam's story, "The Goddess of Revenge," is based on a sensational trial that took place in 1905, when a woman accused of adultery named the men who had used her, many of them eminent and present at the trial; she was not allowed to continue after naming sixty-four of them, and the documents relating to the trial were destroyed by her husband's family.

The truth was that, in casting a new system of private and personal law, the British studied "the scriptures" (as they termed the Vedas) and based the law upon Brahminical tradition, thus forging a powerful alliance between the new laws and an idea of the past that excluded local practices—e.g., the matrilineal system of the Nairs of Kerala—and extended over regions and castes that had had their own nonscriptural local laws and customs. Muslim law was "defined" and contained in a similar manner, often depriving women of what authority they had traditionally had.

Certainly there was a general agreement that education was a necessity for women, but there was a great deal of debate and controversy over what precisely constituted a suitable curriculum and, while the lawmakers were eager to devise a single system to suit all, it was actually the urban middle class that they had in view. Reformists wished to educate women to become "rational" beings in the Western sense, while traditionalists dreaded newfangled Western ways. Nor could they reasonably look to Western women for models. (There was the case of Cornelia Sorabji [1866–1954], who took the examination in law at Oxford in the face of much discouragement and opposition, but was not "called to the Bar" until thirty years later, in 1923, when women were finally admitted there.) Mokshodhyani Mukhopadhyay (c. 1848–?) wrote a hilarious satire on the Bengali *babu* aping Western ways ("He's transported with pride at the thought of his rank— / But faced with a sahib, he trembles in fear! . . . / He flounders while speaking, and stumbles and stutters / But he's speaking in English, you must come and / hear!"), and argued that women in the West were not "free" but had "lost their dignity"; what women needed, she said, was not freedom but access to higher learning.

A large number of the journals and autobiographies collected here record the efforts of women to educate themselves—e.g., Rassundari Debi (1810–?), who taught herself to read and write by borrowing her children's schoolbooks, a page at a time, and scratching the letters of the alphabet onto the blackened kitchen wall of her village home—and to teach others. Savithribai and Jotiba Phule started a school for low-caste girls in Maharashtra, and one of their students, Muktabai, in 1855 at the age of fourteen, wrote a fierce attack upon the Vedas for cruelty to women and *sudras* (lower caste):

> Now obviously, if the Vedas are only for the brahmins, they are absolutely not for us. . . . Let that religion, where only one person is privileged and the rest are deprived, perish from the earth

and let it never enter our minds to be proud of such a religion.

Rokeya Sakhawat Hossain (1880–1932) is only now receiving the recognition she deserved as the author of the first utopian fantasy by an Indian woman, "Sultana's Dream" (1905), in which the astonished—and pleased—narrator visits a land where men have been confined to the *zenana* (women's quarters) by a piece of gentle trickery so that women might move about the cities freely and without veils, where women run the affairs of state in a fraction of the time it takes men since they do not stop for coffee and cigarettes, where solar power keeps the cities clean and free of pollution and transport is provided by aerial conveyances which use hydrogen balls to overcome gravity and electricity to move their wing-like blades. Rokeya Sakhawat Hossain was working on an essay, "The Rights of Women," when she died.

Nationalism is generally considered to have played a major role in the emancipation of Indian women, and it is true that the civil disobedience movement launched by Gandhi brought out large numbers from the seclusion of their homes to join demonstrations of protest. Gandhi's choice of symbols of resistance—the spinning wheel and a pinch of salt—raised these common household objects to an exalted level. There are those, however, who saw the choice as strategic and not idealistic, and some argued that if he was idealizing anything it was domesticity and the place of women in the household. It is a curious fact that during the period when nationalism replaced social issues as the central point of interest, few women wrote on the subject. The nationalist leader Sarojini Naidu (1879–1949) continued to write lyrical and romantic poetry (although she also gave stirring speeches at nationalist gatherings, one of which is included here), and Mahadevi Varma (1907–1987) hardly ever referred to the political events of the time in her poetry and fiercely defended her belief that subjectivity alone was the basis of art.

What was important was how the portrayal of women changed in the literature of the nineteenth century. They were no longer presented as oppressed and uneducated, but as guardians of the nation's spirit, and women felt empowered thereby. The popular Bengali novelist Bankimchandra Chatterjee (1838–1894), in *Devi Chaudhurani*, created a heroine who was "a robber queen with an almost demonic power," but the tensions and conflicts involved were most fully and subtly illustrated in the novels of Rabindranath Tagore. In *The Home and the World* Bimala is seen as embodying the spirit of Mother India and is also referred to as the goddess Durga, but runs into disaster and tragedy when she steps out of her home into the arena of politics. In *Char Adhyaya* there is more explicit criticism of militancy in women:

> At last I see a real girl ... you reign in the home with a fan in your hand and preside over the serving of milk, rice and fish. When you appear with wild hair and angry eyes on the arena where

politics has the whiphand, you are not your normal self but unbalanced, unnatural.

No wonder women fell silent and felt confused:
Were they to be modern and progressive, or traditional
and nationalist? Modernization required criticism of
tradition, while nationalism demanded its glorifica-
tion. Compared to her quandary, that of Western
women in the nineteenth century seems simplicity
itself. (The editors, in fact, are highly critical of
Western feminism for excluding issues of race and
empire and failing to enlarge the scope of insurgency
and resistance.)

There is a school of opinion that says the feminist
question did not "disappear" under nationalism but
was "resolved" by it: nationalism asked that in the
material field Western ideas should reign, and in the
spiritual field Indian; a balance was required between
"the inner and the outer," "the home and the world."
A balance or an irrationally divided personality? No
wonder that women's writing in the 1920s and 1940s
concerns itself with the creation of a resilient self
within the turmoil of changing times. As the critic
Meenakshi Mukherjee puts it, a heroine had to be created who was not merely a good housekeeper but with
whom the hero could plausibly fall in love. Popular literature concerns itself with such a heroine, and it is
realistic rather than escapist. Women readers identified
with it, as is shown by the large number of women's
magazines and journals in all the regional languages.

A review is of necessity reductive. It is to the credit of

the editors of *Women Writing in India* that they never simplify the issues and situations but convey the full complexity and heterogeneity of Indian life. In an introduction that is intellectually rigorous, challenging, and analytical, they recount the adventures of exploring territory that had been lost or forgotten, and rediscovering authors by reading social histories and biographies, yellowed newspapers and legal documents in scattered archives. Libraries had not always preserved the books they owned so that pages were too brittle or faded or moth-eaten to reproduce and had to be copied by hand; in one instance, the library had just sold what the editor was looking for as junk. They also had bits of luck—meeting someone who was able to recite an entire poem they needed (Sr. Mary Begina's "Farewell to the World") and discovering that the ghost in *The Goddess of Revenge* was based on an actual person whose history they tracked down in newspaper reports of her trial. Getting biographical information was equally hard and serendipitous. Often even the children of the writers did not know their dates of birth or death—and knew them only as mothers who "also" wrote—while some writers were too poor or discouraged to have kept copies of their books. What is regarded as history by one age is not necessarily considered so by another: as the editors remind us, the biographies of Buddhist nuns of the sixth century BC provided information about their previous lives and recorded the occasions when they had achieved enlightenment and release from the cycle of birth and death, but nothing else. Testimonials were often colored by the thinking

of their times: a writer would be praised not for her
achievements but because she did not lose "the modesty or sensitivity natural to women" or because education did not "alienate her from her Hindu roots."

Out of the initial list of six hundred, the editors
chose 140 writers, in eleven of the Indian languages.
Problems of translation then arose, but they remained
doggedly ambitious: not content with the usual transla-
tor's aim of a rendering faithful to the original that also
reads well, they

> tried . . . to strain against the reductive and often
> stereotypical homogenization involved in this
> process. We preferred translations that did not
> domesticate the work either into a pan-Indian or
> into a "universalist" mode, but demanded of the
> reader too a translation of herself into another
> sociohistorical ethos. We have taken pains, there-
> fore, to preserve the regional grain of the work,
> and to create a historical context that might open
> the text up for a materialist and feminist reading.

Aware of the foreign readership the book is likely to
attract, their decision to do without a glossary is debat-
able, but not their seriousness of purpose in asking the
reader to "learn slowly, as she relates to the objects, the
concerns, the logic of the worlds women have inhabited over the years, to *live* a mode of life, and not just
read about it." This of course brings them close to soci-
ology or Orientalism, both of which they are anxious
to avoid as being "colonial disciplines," and might

have influenced their decision to do without elaborate transliterations.

One cannot help feeling a glossary would have helped in acquiring that "logic of the worlds ... a mode of life." Certainly an index worthy of the name is required in place of the totally inadequate one provided. The "headnotes" containing biographical material are invaluable since they also provide one with the historical and cultural background of the texts, but one wishes claims such as "the greatest," "the finest," and "the best" were not made quite so often since they are not always borne out—e.g., Swarnakumari Devi does not reveal the talent claimed for her, while the popular writer Ashapurna Debi, criticized for not carrying her feminist views to radical conclusions, contributes a splendidly funny, lively, and spirited short story, "On With the Show," that makes such criticism superfluous. The absence of Toru Dutt from the collection is inexplicable, and it is sad that the editors did not feel they could include the work of Attia Hosain, one of whose short stories would have beautifully illustrated precisely those conflicts and tensions between the upper and the lower classes, the colonizers and the colonized, the modern and the traditional, that they have labored to display.

These are minor bones, perhaps, to pick in a meal where the meat is so satisfying. One can say that the editors and their large team of assistants and advisers have put together a book that is revolutionary, and presents a view of Indian life and history never coherently put together before, and which it will be impossible ever again to ignore. It will be considered a landmark no matter where feminism might take Indian women in the future.

The Feminist Press, by its collaboration on *Truth Tales* with the Kali for Women Press of India, appears to have made a sincere commitment to bring to light precisely such literature as Susie Tharu and K. Lalita wish to make known in *Women Writing in India*. *Truth Tales* is, as a collection, a miniature compared to their mammoth anthology; it consists of a mere seven stories, but they are dense with those customs, manners, and objects that usually remain locked within regional languages because translation robs them of their flavors, tones, and rhythms without clarifying what can seem so mysteriously alien. Some of the translations are more successful than others—the raw vigor and bitter sarcasm of Mahasveta Devi's "The Wet Nurse" come across, and so does the defiant jauntiness of Mrinal Pande's teenager in "Tragedy, in a Minor Key," although much detail will remain obscure. The one story in English, "Midnight Soldiers," reveals that the problem lies not only in language but in tone: in India it would be read as brutally realistic, in the West it appears loaded with melodramatic excess. All require of the reader that effort "to *live* a mode of life, and not just read about it." Those who make the effort will understand why Meena Alexander, in her introduction, says, "The place prescribed for women becomes a fault line, a site of potential rupture."

Anita Desai

- - - - -

DAMSELS

IN

DISTRESS

INEVITABLY, THE SEQUEL to a book that has delighted its readers by its discoveries and its fresh insights and visions will disappoint when it does not repeat its achievement. When we come to the second volume of *Women Writing in India*,[1] the ground has already been broken, the pioneering zest has become familiar, and what had astonished us by its novelty and courage can begin to seem labored and excessive. On hearing the same voices, the same arguments, the ear ceases to register all the shades and tones.

In their preface to the first volume the editors claimed that their anthology was "a joyous retrieval of artifacts that signify women's achievement" and they fulfilled their promise by presenting such lost or unknown gems as the songs of the Buddhist nuns of the sixth century BC; the poetry of bhakti—divine love—rendered in glowingly erotic terms by the Sangam poets of 100 BC–250 AD; the journals in

---

1. *Vol. II: The Twentieth Century*, edited by Susie Tharu and K. Lalita (The Feminist Press at the City University of New York, 1993).

Persian of the Moghul emperor Humayun's sister
Gul-badan Begum; the remarkable autobiography of
Bahinabai, a woman mystic of the seventeenth century; the fourteen-year-old Muktabai's eloquent tirade
against the cruelty and injustice of the Brahmins; the
impertinent fun made of "The Bengali Babu" in verse;
several lively and witty folk songs; the autobiography
of Binodini Das, an actress and theater owner; and
Sultana's Dream, the first utopian fantasy written by an
Indian woman.

In the second volume, alas, we are limited to the
literature of this century and must trudge many a
dreary mile, each sadly like the other, with exceptional
or distinguished work only occasionally lighting our
way. Where, in all this agony and lament, is the spirit,
the courage, and sheer creative force that illuminate
so much of the Indian scene and of which we find evidence everywhere? It is in the color and fantasy displayed on mud walls, dusty thresholds, rag quilts, and
silk weavings. It is present in song and dance, in family
and community life, in fairs, festivals, pilgrimages,
ceremonies, and rituals. Women have kept alive in
language a sharpness of wit and inventiveness and a
heritage of myth, proverb, and legend. Has the twentieth century succeeded in totally eroding all these? And
what of the feel and savor of ordinary, everyday life,
not life when lived at its highest pitch, but when it is
merely sober and commonplace? One searches in the
volume under review for a glimpse of these experiences, and begins to doubt one's own memory, but
one is brought up short by the editors' stern announce-

ment that "there will be few gratifications here," and
for several reasons:

> The refurbishment of canons was not the primary
> task we ourselves addressed. Had the recovery of
> literature, lost or damned in the conduit of male
> criticism, been our major interest, we might have
> translated different authors, made somewhat dif-
> ferent selections, and used different working
> norms. . . .
>
> We have not, then, simply tried to make good
> the loss for literary studies. The interests of that
> monumental institution as it stands are ones we
> wish to transform, not entrench. . . .
>
> If we restrain ourselves from enthusiastically
> recovering women's writing to perform the same
> services to society and to nation that mainstream
> literature over the last hundred years has been
> called upon to do, we might learn to read compo-
> sitions . . . not for the moments in which they col-
> lude with or reinforce dominant ideologies of
> gender, class, nation, or empire, but for the ges-
> tures of defiance or subversion implicit in them.

These "gestures of defiance and subversion" that the
editors have traced in a dozen different languages—
Marathi, Oriya, Urdu, Telugu, Kannada, Bengali,
Hindi, etc.—make story after story and poem after
poem ring with the wail of the woman scorned, the
lament of the woman humiliated or dispossessed, the
keening of women in distress; and the finger of blame is

pointed not only at the patriarchy but at the wider world of power and imperialism that the editors, Susie Tharu and K. Lalita, feel that Western feminists such as Elaine Showalter, Sandra Gilbert, and Susan Gubar have paid insufficient attention to and have not studied or understood as Indian feminists have.

In recounting the history of women's struggles in India, the editors' labor is as thorough, painstaking, and single-minded as in the earlier volume. If we are to study women's literature (how bourgeois a term and concept in this context!) in order to discover "how the efforts of these women shaped the worlds we inherited, and what, therefore, is the history, not of authority, but of contest and engagement we can claim today," and if we are also to ask, "What was the price they paid in these transactions, what did they concede, and how do those costs and concessions affect our inheritance"— then the study of the history and politics that are both the cause and the effect of such efforts and transactions becomes unavoidable.

Such aims set the editors apart from the feminists and literary critics of the West, and they are acutely aware of the difference:

> We have tried to map the imaginative worlds in which women wrote. We have read their literary initiatives as attempts to engage with the force and the conflict of the multiple, cross-cutting determinations of their historical worlds. Literary criticism, in its authoritative, New Critical mode focuses on the internal structure and

aesthetic achievement of what is taken to be a self-referential, hermetic text. In contrast, our readings have treated women's texts as engaged in negotiation, debate, and protest, inevitably in areas that directly concern, or are closely related to, what it means to be a woman. These texts address real tasks in a real world, and are therefore documents of historical struggles over the making of citizen-selves and nation worlds.

The study is emphatically not intended as one of private citizens and their distinctively personal and spiritual worlds. We are to look at women as "citizens" of a "nation"—words that lead one to questions regarding these two concepts as defined by the freedom movement and its leaders in the twentieth century. B.R. Ambedkar (1891–1956), the author of the Indian constitution, defined nationality as a "subjective psychological feeling. It is the feeling of corporate sentiment of oneness that makes those that are charged with it feel they are kith and kin. . . ." In the words of the editors, "the geography of a nation is not so much territorial as imaginative." The nation, then, is not only a theoretical and political entity but an imaginative concept that is consolidated by its art and culture, which are of course "always being recreated: contested, fractured, elaborated, redistributed, and *rewritten*. . . . Its closures, therefore— . . . are never complete, never total." The Indian constitution provided for universal suffrage and therefore, at least theoretically, women were given an equal part in these activities; but the social structure, with its traditions, actually meant that women found themselves working in the margins, or in opposition to the general current. This was hardly what had been intended.

India had for its first prime minister a man who loved words and whose autobiographical *Discovery of India* has been called one of the "foundational fictions" of the nation. In Nehru's inspiring speech on the "tryst with destiny," made on Independence Day on the ramparts of the Red Fort in Delhi under the fluttering Indian tricolor, he had guaranteed the new nation political and economic self-reliance and the creation of a secular, democratic society. No one noticed, in the euphoria of the moment, the two quite different aspects of the promise: economic growth and independence would require the protection and fostering of the business and landed interests of the bourgeoisie and a new commercial class, and of necessity an imbalanced social structure, whereas the secular, democratic society was to be based on social justice and equality. The Congress Committee Resolution on Economic Policy made the same ambiguous commitment:

> To evolve a political system which will combine efficiency of administration with individual liberty and an economic structure which will yield maximum production without the concentration of private monopolies. . . . Such a social structure can provide an alternative to the acquisitive economy of private capitalism and regimentation of a totalitarian state.

The committee also unequivocally stated that "land, with its mineral resources and other means of production, as well as distribution and exchange must belong to and be regulated by the community in its own interest."

The weaknesses and tensions inherent in this concept had been established and became clearly visible in the Sixties and Seventies. Economic growth, agricultural development, and land reforms ran into problems, slowed, or stalled; the population soared, unemployment rose, prices spiraled, and peasant revolts broke out in different parts of the country. Students and urban intellectuals, traditionally the disaffected, threw in their lot with peasant revolutionaries, and the nation was wracked by violent outbursts, widespread protests, and strikes that paralyzed institutions from the railways to the universities. In 1975 the then prime minister, Indira Gandhi, declared a state of emergency, postponed elections, suspended civil rights, and, for the first time in independent India's history, imposed press censorship. The resistance movement was driven underground and silenced, but only briefly. Mrs. Gandhi's program of enforced slum clearance and compulsory sterilization so enraged the public that the government was toppled: for the first time since Independence it was widely seen as not benign but adversarial, an opponent.

Once again, the editors write, "new forms of Indianness had to be invented, new identities forged for both state and citizen." Women's involvement in recent Indian history is seen by the editors as passing through three distinct phases since the 1900s: first, the program of the freedom movement called Swadeshi ("of one's own country"); second, the Progressive Writers' Association and its dealings with issues of caste and gender; and third, the feminist movement of the Twenties and Thirties as it resurfaced in the Seventies.

Swadeshi was envisaged by Gandhi as a program in which women had a crucial part. His choice of symbols—the spinning wheel that would produce clothing for India's millions and put an end to the import of machine-made cloth from Britain, and the pinch of salt gathered on the seashore that would demonstrate the Indian refusal to pay British taxes—was brilliantly domestic, even feminine. As he hoped, Swadeshi involved the population at every level—folk art and crafts were revived, folk music played and sung, a village economy was encouraged, and local festivals were imbued with nationalistic ardor and celebrated.

Of course such a program selected what it was to revive, and often what was "revived" was an imaginary, or legendary, historical or religious phenomenon. When the poet-philosopher Aurobindo Ghosh (1872–1950) wrote of "a single and living religious spirit" he referred to Hindu spirit, for he went on to hope it would "Aryanize the world." At the same time V. D. Savarkar, in his treatise *Hindutva*, presented his notion of the "Hindu *rashtra*" or Hindu state. The popular Bengali novelist Bankimchandra Chatterjee (1838–1894) wrote abusively of all foreigners—British and Muslim—in his acclaimed historical novels. The creation of the Indian "Self" was also creating the "Other"—a concept that has acquired monstrous proportions in today's Hindu fundamentalist movement.

The next phase of political—and feminist—activity was influenced by the Progressive Writers' Association and the Indian People's Theater Association, and many of the women represented in the anthology belonged to one or the other. Joining these organizations between 1920 and the mid-1940s would have changed their lives, making them less domestic and more public, and would have put many women in touch with the wider community, giving them a sense of their responsibilities and importance. They wrote plays and took them on tours to villages and cities. They organized book clubs and discussion groups, studied folk music and theater, and consciously addressed social issues in their writing. Involvement with trade unions and peasant struggles transformed the lives of these middle-class urban intellectuals, but the literature they produced remained that of their class: the urban middle-class intellectual. After Independence, many of these activities lost their sense of direction as they were drawn into national programs for literature and theater, and state academies were set up under state patronage.

At the same time, the urge women felt to organize in order to achieve goals that remained elusive— education, better health and maternity care, the abolition of practices such as child marriage, dowry, and purdah—grew in strength. The All India Women's Conference could influence government policy and did so consistently. There were some within the ranks, however, who felt there were "contradictions between the interests of women and the interests of Congress nationalists." One worker at the AIWC said that men had

> welcomed the women into the struggle and honoured them because they wanted their help at this moment, but when women contest for seats at elections, when women come forward to contest places of honour and emoluments, it will be quite different; it will be a fight between the sexes. Further, under our present social system, it will be an unequal fight.

She was right about the inequality but wrong about what was to be gained, which proved not to be seats or honor—Indian women have had both—but merely daily bread and a living.

For all the activities and efforts of women's organizations, the texts in this anthology testify that the lot of Indian women has remained depressingly the same. Domination by the father and the husband, the stranglehold of the social community or caste, illiteracy, ill health, dire and grinding poverty, slavish conditions of domestic life, the injustices of the dowry system and arranged marriages, unhygienic childbirth, unwanted pregnancies, and unremitting suffering—these are themes of the stories and accounts collected here; there are no others.

Although the AIWC became less active after Independence was won, its work had to be continued and is now largely in the hands of NGOs—nongovernmental organizations—working with women in rural, tribal, and also heavily industrialized areas, often through unions and cooperatives (as in other times through schools and clinics). Many of the stories here are informed by such experience. The editors have drawn a parallel between the "consciousness-raising" groups of women in the West and the "speaking bitterness" campaigns of the Chinese cultural revolution. Both are suggested in the writing collected in the present anthology, although here it is the individual that speaks. Can individual compositions really substitute for group expression and perform the same function? There are inherent tensions in such an undertaking. The editors warn against such work being endorsed by feminists as "*women's* experiences" that are part of a "female" tradition with a presumed affinity with peace or nature or the unconscious. They have no admiration for the enthusiastic circulation of such ideas among third world scholars. They urge their readers to study their selection of texts

> not as new *monuments* to existing institutions . . . but as *documents* that display what is at stake in the embattled practices of self and agency, and in the making of a habitable world, at the margins of patriarchies reconstituted by the emerging bourgeoisies of empire and nation. . . . We are interested in how the efforts of these women shaped the worlds we inherited, and what, therefore, is the history, not of authority, but of contest and engagement we claim today.

This lengthy, and weighty, introduction forms our guide to the texts. Clutching it, we make our way across the map laid out for us with such clarity and precision. But it can help us only so far and no further. Eventually we must wade into the literature and then our responses can be no more than individual and subjective. Often the information provided to guide the reader will seem confusing and even misleading; its relation to the texts is not always so obvious and biographical notes for each writer are written without the discernment and scrupulousness displayed in the introduction. Typical entries read:

> Vatsala used the inaccessible hills of Wyanad and its fertile soil as a symbolic backdrop to present the loves and frustrations of a people untouched by modern civilization. Hidden within those silent hills were sad stories of the exploitation of the virgin soil and of virgin women. No other novelist has captured the topography of Wyanad so accurately.

and

> Among those who have influenced her work, she cites Friedrich Nietzsche, Carl Jung, Jean-Paul Sartre, and Franz Kafka. Her themes, like those of many of her contemporaries, are alienation, loneliness, ennui, and the existential predicament.

The latter entry is followed by the lines:

Mine once the flowers of lips speaking,
Now turned stony seals.
Mine now the whirlpools of your mind,
The unfinished chapters of your life,
The bitterness of your days.
The vehemence of your passions.

The thorns in your path hurt my feet,
The pangs of your heart strike my ribs too ...

This is only too typical of most of the poetry included here. Sugatha Kumari's poem goes:

Night rain
Like some young madwoman
Weeping, laughing, whimpering
For nothing
Muttering without a stop ...

Even verse by a well-known film star, Meena Kumari, is included—more for the sake of her personal allure, one feels ("an exceptionally beautiful and talented actress, always dressed in white") than for such lines as: "The spattering, singing drops of rain / Hold poison and immortality too ... "

One turns to the prose and finds that most of the stories deal with the woeful widow, the abused daughter-in-law, the neglected grandmother. Such a collection creates a portrait of a long-suffering creature who is dragged through life only by her sense of duty and self-sacrifice. It is true that some women do manage to make the "gestures of defiance and subversion" the editors promise us, sometimes only after their deaths, when they come back to haunt the wicked living. In "The Blanket" the avaricious modern young woman deprives her poor old mother-in-law of a beautiful imported blanket sent her by her son. She then finds she falls ill with a high fever when she sleeps under it and recovers only when she gives it away to a beggar woman. In "Life Sentence" the husband who thought he was doing a woman a favor by marrying her feels remorse after her death for her silent subjection to a lifetime of hard labor and self-denial. He says, "Only when I see newly married couples, I yearn to be born a second time and to marry Janaki again."

In such circumstances, quite small incidents can acquire great significance. In Mrinal Pande's "Fellow Travelers" an unhappy widow reaches the breaking point and expresses it by smacking her small son. But the opportunity for full-blooded revenge, calculated and deliberate, is given to few; a rare instance occurs in Wajeda Tabassum's "Castoffs," in which a servant girl, tired of wearing her rich mistress's worn-out clothing, seduces the young man who is to marry her just before the wedding. For once her mistress will experience what it is like to have what is cast off by another.

Curiously for an anthology with an openly political agenda, there is no mention in any of the texts of the major political events and circumstances in India during this century—British colonialism and the freedom movement. The editors themselves comment on this absence, but do not acknowledge the copious literature about them, for example in Raja Rao's *Kanthapura* and *The Cow of the Barricades*, R.K. Narayan's *Waiting for the Mahatma*, and Salman Rushdie's *Midnight's Children*. And if one is to keep to women's writing, one could mention Attia Hosain's *Sunlight on a Broken Column*, Kamala Markandaya's earlier novels, Nayantara Sahgal's fiction and autobiography, Qurrutulain Hyder's *River of Fire*, Bapsi Sidhwa's *Cracking India*, to name just a few. Avoiding the "mainstream" is not always a rewarding policy to follow.

Easily the most interesting work to be found here has no literary pretensions or ambitions whatever. In "I'm Telling You, Listen," the Marathi actress Hamsa Wadkar conceals nothing in her plain and prosaic account of her life. She was the granddaughter of a courtesan, married an older man, suffered his beatings and punishments, supported his family and hers. She ran away to become the second wife of another man but returned, and eventually sank into alcoholism and solitude. Dudala Salamma, an illiterate peasant woman who fought in the Telangana People's Struggle between 1946 and 1951 and whose oral testimony was collected by a women's group seeking out the history of the women who took part in the struggle, tells her story complete with "the pauses, the waverings, the incoherence" of her original testimony.

> You ask why I did feed them? Why have you come here to see me? Why do you roam about, for the Sangham or for women? I too wanted to do the same thing. At least you can read a few letters, but

me, I used to graze buffaloes. I lived in the strength
and faith that a communist survives on the
strength of the shoulder. The struggle for fuel and
water—I lived in such strength and power for it.

Also included is the autobiographical account of
Baby Kamble, a *mahar* or untouchable, who describes
the life of her caste and its efforts to gain entry to temples and access to village wells.

Of course such work comes close to the "anthropol-
ogy" that the editors despise as a tool of imperialism
and the colonizer's power. They refuse to treat it as such
and avoid the glossaries that might, for some, seem to
place it within that category. Sometimes the lack of
such a glossary makes for incomprehensible reading,
even when it comes to fiction: Anupama Niranjana's
story "The Incident—and After" is full of such phrases
as "signed the letter with her mangalsutra" [her wedding necklace] and refers to a young man "pulling off
his trousers" on entering his mother's room. In a book
compiled for a Western, English-speaking audience,
this surely requires explanation: he is going to get into
more comfortable clothing such as a *dhoti or lungi*.

The collaboration of the editors and The Feminist
Press has proved its worth in the two volumes of
Women Writing in India. Perhaps their next venture
should be into oral history, or autobiography, or letters
and journals, material that lends itself much more
tractably to their purposes than do fiction and poetry,
which will not bend and remain stubbornly what they
are—good or bad, but themselves.

Roderick MacFarquhar

- - - - -

India:

The Imprint

of Empire

1

- - - - -

IN 1947, ON the eve of Indian independence, my parents arranged for me to fly from Britain for what promised to be our last family holiday in the subcontinent. As a British member of the Indian Civil Service, my father expected to leave with the departing Raj.[1] My mother and I drove up from New Delhi to the Vale of Kashmir. We visited my brother's grave in Srinagar, where he had died in infancy a decade earlier, one of an estimated two million graves the British left behind. Then we trekked the final 2,000 feet on tiny ponies up to Gulmarg, where my father joined us after attending the Indian independence ceremonies in New Delhi on August 15. It was an idyllic holiday, Raj-style: golf on two of the most beautiful courses in the world, where the ball soared encouragingly far in the thin mountain air; picnics among the firs and pines; bridge in the club;

---

1. According to Philip Woodruff, *The Men Who Ruled India, I: The Founders; II: The Guardians* (London: Jonathan Cape, 1953, 1954), in 1939 there were 1,384 officers in the ICS, of whom 759 were British expatriates (II, p. 363). After partition, my father went to Karachi to work for the new Pakistani government.

the latest Agatha Christie mystery in the evening before turning in.

But on the plains of the Punjab, where I had grown up, one of the greatest human tragedies of the twentieth century was taking place. The proudest province of British India, which had just been partitioned between the successor states, India and Pakistan, was collapsing into a state of nature. Sikhs and Hindus killed their Muslim neighbors; Muslims killed Sikhs and Hindus. Millions of Hindus and Sikhs fled eastward to India, Muslims westward to Pakistan.[2] Hundreds of thousands didn't make it.

Trainloads of refugees were ambushed and boarded before they reached the border, and their occupants slaughtered to a man, woman, and child.[3] Only the engine driver would be left alive so that he could deliver his grisly cargo across the border.[4]

---

2. According to the 1941 census, the undivided Punjab consisted of 52.88 percent Muslims, 29.79 percent Hindus, and 14.62 percent Sikhs; Indu Banga, editor, *Five Punjabi Centuries: Policy, Economy, Society, and Culture, c. 1500–1990* (New Delhi: Manohar, 1997), p. 243.

3. Philip Ziegler, *Mountbatten: The Official Biography* (Collins, 1985), p. 437, and Larry Collins and Dominique Lapierre, *Freedom at Midnight* (Simon and Schuster, 1975), p. 342, quote estimates of the dead ranging from 200,000 to 500,000; J. S. Grewal, *The Sikhs of the Punjab* (Cambridge University Press, 1990), p. 181, and Patrick French, *Liberty or Death: India's Journey to Independence and Division* (HarperCollins, 1997), p. 349, agree on a million. The highest figure I have seen is "almost" or "over" 2,000,000 in Akbar S. Ahmed, *Jinnah, Pakistan and Islamic Identity: The Search for Saladin* (Routledge, 1997) pp. xi, 166. Estimates of the number of refugees who managed to survive the two-way border crossing in the Punjab and elsewhere range from 8,000,000 to as high as 17,000,000.

4. For recent accounts of the "ethnic cleansing" of Partition, see S. M. Burke

Rumors began to reach Gulmarg that former
comrades-in-arms of the British Indian Army, now
divided into the armed forces of the new nations, were
about to fall upon each other in the disputed province
of Kashmir. Situated on the Indo-Pakistani border,
Kashmir was supposed to have its future decided by the
maharaja. Since over 75 percent of Kashmiris were
Muslims but the maharaja was a Hindu, both countries
hoped for his adherence. He procrastinated, then opted
for India. No Pakistani leader since has been willing or
able to live with the small portion of Kashmir which his
country retained after the fighting of 1947–1948. And
so, fifty years and three wars later on, a costly arms
race continues, nuclear weapons are developed, missiles are deployed, border clashes take place as I write.[5]

I left Gulmarg on an American plane sent to Srinagar to evacuate embassy staff. Flying low over the
Punjab, we saw villages burning below. In New Delhi,
our house was deserted; the Muslim servants had fled
to refugee camps in the capital. Working as a volunteer,
I saw the pitiful condition of the wounded in one of the
camps. When my parents returned we located our servants and smuggled them out of New Delhi, where

---

and Salim Al-Din Quraishi, *The British Raj in India: An Historical Review*
(Oxford University Press, 1995), pp. 609–625, and French, *Liberty or Death*,
pp. 342–356.

. 5. Prem Shankar Jha, *Kashmir, 1947: Rival Versions of History* (Delhi:
Oxford University Press, 1996). For a scalding critique of Britain's handling
of its treaty obligations to princely states like Kashmir, see Ian Copland, *The
Princes of India in the Endgame of Empire, 1917–1947* (Cambridge
University Press, 1997).

killings were still taking place, hiding them in the bathroom of our carriage on the train to Bombay, where things were calmer. I sailed home to school.

In the years that followed, I returned often to the subcontinent, but always to examine some current problem. "What's gone wrong with us now?" my friends used to ask plaintively. Going back to New Delhi for the fiftieth anniversary of Independence this summer, however, it was the scenes of 1947 that were uppermost in my mind. How did Indians look back on the bloodshot moment of Partition which marked the end of British rule?

2
- - - - -

ANSWERS WERE HARD to find; there has not been a German-style soul-searching in the subcontinent. According to the Delhi University historian Gyanendra Pandey, "Indian intellectuals have tended to celebrate the story of the Independence struggle rather than dwell on the agonies of Partition." Pandey lists evident reasons why the Hindu–Muslim violence has had little attention. Bitter conflict between Hindus and Muslims persists in parts of India today; and those who pursue the history of such strife run the real danger of reopening old wounds. In addition, there is no consensus among Indians about the nature of Partition. "We have no means of representing such tragic loss, nor of

pinning down—or rather, owning—responsibility for
it. Consequently, our nationalist historiography, jour-
nalism, and filmmaking have tended to generate something like a collective amnesia."[6]

For the political scientist Ashis Nandy at Delhi's
Center for the Study of Developing Societies, "the silence
was one way known to the South Asians to start life
anew and contain bitterness. It was a means of restoring community life, interpersonal trust and the known
moral universe." Many wanted to wipe away the memories, "both what had been done to them or what was
done or sanctioned by them." Still, Nandy wrote, it is
gradually "becoming obvious that the summer of 1947
brought out the worst in us, so much so that even
our imagination of evil failed." Writing of the "psycho-
pathic and sadistic dimensions of the carnage," he
concluded that Independence meant "genocide, necro-
philia, ethnic cleansing, massive uprooting and collapse of a moral universe."[7]

The implication of such an account is that the
responsibility for the slaughter has to be borne by
"ordinary" Indians and Pakistanis who turned against
each other; the manner of the bloodletting allows of no
other conclusion. But what about the Partition that
sparked it? The "communal" tensions between Hindus
and Muslims in the subcontinent date back centuries

6. Gyanendra Pandey, "In Defense of the Fragment: Writing about
Hindu–Muslim Riots in India Today," in Ranajit Guha, editor, A Subaltern
Studies Reader, 1986–1995 (University of Minnesota Press, 1997).

7. Ashis Nandy, "Too Painful for Words," The Times of India, July 20, 1997.

to the successive waves of Muslim conquerors who swept down through the Khyber Pass and forced their Hindu subjects to convert. In the twentieth century, some Muslims feared religious, cultural, and economic subordination to the Hindu majority, perhaps even revenge for their earlier victories. Their leaders embraced the theory that the subcontinent comprised "two nations," each of which deserved its own homeland; the idea of a unified subcontinent was imposed by the British.

At the same time Indians have long blamed British divide-and-rule policies for exacerbating and entrenching communal barriers. The Raj was certainly Machiavellian from time to time, not to mention blundering and harsh, but closer to the mark was probably the well-known Indian judgment: "We divided and they ruled." In one of the articles for the fiftieth anniversary, Nitesh Sengupta blamed the British for not conceding home rule after World War I when the future founder of Pakistan, M. A. Jinnah, was still a loyal member of the Indian National Congress.[8]

Sengupta, however, blamed the Congress for the political missteps that occurred thereafter. For instance, in June 1946 Nehru told a press conference that the central government of an independent India (which would be dominated by his Congress Party) would reserve its rights to intervene in the component states of

---

8. Nitish Sengupta, "Partition need not have happened if. . . ," *The Times of India*, August 6, 1997. Sengupta is the director general of the International Management Institute, New Delhi.

the union on issues of planning and economic development. (India was ultimately to be divided into twenty-
five states and centrally administered territories.) Since
the Congress had earlier accepted a three-tier constitutional arrangement designed to allow Muslims to exercise all powers in their regions except for defense,
foreign affairs, and communications, Jinnah regarded
Nehru's assertion as treachery. According to Sengupta,
only the final nail in the coffin of a united independent
India was driven by the British, when Mountbatten
arrived as Britain's last viceroy and decided to acceler-
ate Britain's departure by ten months. It is over this issue
that British historians have been arguing.

Essentially, the case against Mountbatten, apart from
justifiable jibes about his relentless self-glorification—
"I was governing by personality," he later told Nehru's
authorized biographer—is that he was pro-Indian and
anti-Pakistan, pro-Nehru and anti-Jinnah. He put pressure on the supposedly neutral Boundary Commissioner,
Sir Cyril Radcliffe, to make critical adjustments in
favor of India when drawing the frontier through
the Punjab. A Cambridge don of Pakistani origin has
asserted that "if Jinnah is the first Pakistani, Mountbatten is the first Paki-basher." Mountbatten and his
wife certainly hit it off instantly with Nehru, while the
viceroy later made it clear that he had found Jinnah
impossible to deal with.[9]

157

---

9. Nehru and the Mountbattens had similar leftish political outlooks, and
there is the imponderable importance of the undeniably affectionate relationship between the Indian premier and Edwina Mountbatten.

Cyril Radcliffe had no expert knowledge of India. He was given a task of Solomonic proportions to be completed in an irresponsibly short period of time. He was not insulated from lobbying as claimed but was in contact with Mountbatten and his staff. But since Radcliffe destroyed all his papers on returning to England we cannot know if his earlier ideas on the Punjab boundary were modified by common sense or by the Congress Party via Mountbatten. Auden's caustic poem on his performance remains one of the most telling commentaries written on the Partition.

> *"Time," they had briefed him in London, "is short.*
>   *It's too late*
> *For mutual reconciliation or rational debate:*
> *The only solution now lies in separation.*
> *The Viceroy thinks, as you will see from his letter,*
> *That the less you are seen in his company the better,*
> *So we've arranged to provide you with other*
>   *accommodation . . . "*
> *Shut up in a lonely mansion, with police night*
>   *and day*
> *Patrolling the gardens to keep assassins away,*
> *He got down to work, to the task of settling the fate*
> *Of millions. The maps at his disposal were out*
>   *of date*
> *And the Census Returns almost certainly incorrect,*
> *But there was no time to check them, no time*
>   *to inspect*
> *Contested areas. The weather was frightfully hot,*

And a bout of dysentery kept him constantly
    on the trot,
But in seven weeks it was done, the frontiers decided,
A continent for better or worse divided.
The next day he sailed for England, where he
    quickly forgot
The case, as a good lawyer must.
    Return he would not,
Afraid, as he told his Club, that he might get shot.

The second set of charges against Mountbatten is that by deciding in June 1947 to advance the date of Independence from June 1948 to August 1947, he left no time for further negotiation and therefore made Partition inevitable. This also ensured that the exchange of populations would be hurried, chaotic, and bloody. He delayed announcing the location of Radcliffe's boundaries until after Independence, at which point the responsibility for law and order devolved on India and Pakistan. He did so, it is alleged, because he sensed a PR disaster in the making for himself and Britain. So, disastrously, there was no British-led unified Indian Army to oversee the transfer of populations. It was issues like these that led Kuldip Nayar, a leading columnist and former High Commissioner in London, to suggest holding a joint Indo-Pakistani seminar to mark the fiftieth anniversary entitled "The Trial of Mountbatten."

How he would have emerged from a fair trial remains unknowable. Mountbatten was an energetic and charismatic viceroy, if often guilty of gross errors of judgment. His colleague Field Marshal Sir Gerald Templer once commented: "You're so crooked, Dickie, if you swallowed a nail you'd shit a corkscrew." Yet many knowledgeable British officials with no cause to admire him felt that in the light of the deteriorating communal situation in the spring of 1947, Britain had no alternative but to hand over power as soon as possible; further delay would have spread the massacres beyond the Punjab to all of India. Moreover, although Mountbatten claimed credit for advancing the timetable, the decision was actually taken in the India Office in London.[10]

Whatever the verdict of history, Mountbatten undoubtedly charmed the Indian public. On the occasion of the Mountbattens' departure for England in June 1948, Nehru remarked how struck he had been at the reception given them in old Delhi earlier in the day:

> [Used] as I am to these vast demonstrations here, I was much affected, and I wondered how it was that an Englishman and Englishwoman could

---

10. The case for the defense is given principally by the official biographer, Philip Ziegler, in whom Mountbatten has been fortunate: *Mountbatten*, pp. 349–379, and especially pp. 438–441; Collins and Lapierre, *Freedom at Midnight*, gave Mountbatten the opportunity to state his own case; French, *Liberty or Death*, pp. 305, 443, note 45, takes a more objective view, but rejects the notion that a premature British departure was a primary cause of the massacres. Andrew Roberts, in a chapter titled "Lord Mountbatten and the perils of adrenalin" in his *Eminent Churchillians* (Simon and Schuster, 1994), pp. 55–136, attacks Mountbatten's character vigorously and presents a caustic exposé of the egregious errors which he contends littered his entire career; the famous quote from Templer is on page 133.

become so popular during this brief period of time.... Obviously this was not connected so much with what had happened, but rather with the good faith, the friendship and the love of India that these two possessed....

Obviously, too, that friendship helped Nehru decide to keep India within the Commonwealth even when it became a republic, thus ensuring that most British ex-colonies followed suit and giving post-imperial Britain the illusion of retaining its global stature. Three decades later, long after Mountbatten's friends and contemporaries of the Independence era had died, when the IRA blew up his fishing boat, killing him and members of his family, the Indian parliament and state assemblies stopped their proceedings, shops closed, and a week's state mourning was declared.

3

- - - - -

AS INDIA SHOWED, the end of empire is never easy. The older imperial powers were crippled economically by World War II and lost their aura of unchallengeable authority. In the early postwar years, the British were fortunate to be led by a Labour Party committed to decolonization. Some nations learned the hard way that "nerve without muscle," as the historian Lawrence James put it, could not save an empire.[11] In the fifty years that followed the end of the Raj, virtually the entire British empire in Asia, Africa, and the Americas was dismantled, sometimes peacefully, sometimes with bitterness and bloodshed.[12] During the same period, the other European empires—French, Dutch, Portuguese, Belgian, Spanish—also largely disappeared, and the US left the Philippines.[13] Even the Soviet and tsarist empires collapsed. It was the greatest liberation of subject peoples in history.

The process culminated on June 30 this year with the return to China of Hong Kong, the last great jewel in the tattered imperial regalia of Europe. No imperial divestiture had been longer in the making, but probably not since the loss of the American colonies had the British elite been so publicly and venomously divided about a retreat from empire as it took place. And though Britain had certainly never left a colony in as good economic shape as Hong Kong, there was continual wrangling between the outgoing and incoming sovereigns, which readers of *The New York Review* have had a chance to consider in detail.[14] For the student of the end

---

11. See his *The Rise and Fall of the British Empire* (London: Abacus, 1995), p. 555.

12. For an interesting "worm's-eye view" of this process, see Robin Neillands, *A Fighting Retreat: The British Empire, 1947–1997* (London: Coronet, 1997).

13. See John Keay, *Last Post: The End of Empire in the Far East* (London: John Murray, 1997). Kipling's "The White Man's Burden" was written to encourage the American effort in the Philippines; Rudyard Kipling, *Complete Verse: Definitive Edition* (Anchor, 1989), pp. 321–323.

14. Among other articles, see, for example, Ian Buruma, "Holding Out in Hong Kong," *The New York Review*, June 12, 1997, and Jonathan Mirsky, "Betrayal," *The New York Review*, September 25, 1997.

of empire, the question is: Why did Hong Kong 1997 arouse so much sound and fury while India 1947 did not?

In 1947, although disasters were foreseen, there was little time for reflection—even the high priest of the imperial mission, Churchill, finally accepted that there was no alternative to granting independence to the Indian subcontinent. But in 1997, there persisted to the very end, and at the highest levels, the uneasy feeling that Britain was not behaving honorably. Prime Minister Thatcher later said she hated signing the Joint Declaration of 1984 that sentenced Hong Kong citizens to live under a Communist dictatorship. But in 1989, in the aftermath of the Tiananmen massacre, she rejected a proposal made by Governor Sir David Wilson to grant full British passports to the three and a half million people in the colony who ranked as British Dependent Territories Citizens. The specter, however unlikely, of a flood of refugees from Hong Kong was politically intolerable.

After John Major replaced Mrs. Thatcher, Foreign Office experts persuaded him to go to Beijing to sign an agreement on Hong Kong's new airport. He was embarrassed to become the first Western leader to shake hands with Premier Li Peng, widely despised in the West for his role in Tiananmen. Somewhat unjustly, Major decided to make Wilson, not Sir Percy Cradock, his principal adviser on China policy, the scapegoat for the position he'd been put in. By this time, the new foreign secretary, Douglas Hurd, had become convinced that the endgame in Hong Kong demanded the presence of a political heavyweight rather than a

Foreign Office mandarin. Out went Sir David in digni-
fied silence and in came the ex–cabinet minister Chris
Patten, chastened by his personal electoral defeat, but
ebullient about his new job.

Patten, like Mountbatten, had two enormous ad-
vantages over his predecessor, a direct line to the prime
minister—who attributed his continuance in office
after the 1992 general election to Patten's chairman-
ship of the campaign—and to the foreign secretary,
both former cabinet colleagues, and carte blanche to
do what he thought best. By adhering to the letter of
the 1984 Joint Declaration and the Chinese Basic Law
implementing it, if not to their spirit, Patten set out to
further democratize the Hong Kong electoral system.
The British ambassador in Beijing, Sir Robin McLaren,
warned that the Chinese government would react badly,
and it did. The Beijing authorities expected to be handed
a cozy, controllable colonial system with which their
officials would be quite comfortable. Instead, they would
inherit a Legislative Council which they could rightly
anticipate would include significant numbers of capable opponents, such as the barrister Martin Lee.

Before long, Patten was denounced by Beijing pro-
pagandists as a "clown," a "dirty trickster," a "tango
dancer," a "strutting prostitute," a "serpent," an "assassin," and the "criminal of all time." Far more dangerous for Patten was the assault of those whom he called
the "Sinologists," the Foreign Office officials who had
helped shape the policy of cooperation with China that
had produced the Joint Declaration. Clearly it was
galling for them to be depicted in the press as pusillani-

mous appeasers who kowtowed to the Chinese. Cradock denigrated Patten for "incompetence" and self-aggrandizement.[15] But what probably guided the Sinologists most strongly was their conviction that, precisely because the Chinese were "thugs," as Cradock was wont to describe them, the only option was to coax them into the least punitive arrangements for Hong Kong. "Confrontation" would be counterproductive.

Again, there can be no final judgment. But the Sinologists surely underestimated the character of Hong Kong as revealed by the demonstrations of more than a million people there after the Tiananmen crackdown. Hong Kong could no longer be dismissed as an apolitical city, interested only in acquiring wealth. Its citizens were profoundly concerned about the politics of their forthcoming sovereign and deeply worried that the rule of law which had become integral to their political identity might disappear after July 1, 1997. No governor could have guaranteed their future. The Chinese have duly swept aside Patten's reforms and the legislative body which they produced. But Patten provided Hong Kongers with a sense of what they needed to fight for if they were to breathe reality into Deng Xiaoping's concept of "one country, two systems." One of his leading Hong Kong opponents even conceded that he transformed the political culture by introducing open debate and government accountability.

---

15. For the controversy over Cradock's views and activities, see Jonathan Dimbleby, *The Last Governor: Chris Patten and the Handover of Hong Kong* (Little, Brown, 1997), pp. 10, 161, 166–167, 414–415, 436–437, 444–445.

Unlike Mountbatten, Patten did not have the benefit of a moving and affectionate farewell from the new sovereign power. But Patten, too, seems to have become widely popular. Even in his final months, when he was effectively a lame duck, the leading opinion-sampling organization found that 60 percent of the population still supported Patten, a third of them would have liked Hong Kong to remain British or become independent, while 90 percent, the highest percentage ever, admitted to being content with their lives under British rule. The pollsters added that "as the sun sets on British administration in Hong Kong, many aspects of life under [British] rule seem suffused with a 'golden haze.'"[16]

The haze will dissipate. Nobody can long cherish the memory of being a colonial subject.[17] And after the parting comes the reckoning. History will be rewritten in Hong Kong as it was in India, and likely more harshly.[18] China's foreign minister, Qian Qichen, has

---

16. Dimbleby, *The Last Governor*, pp. 417, 435. The understandably schizophrenic feelings of Hong Kong citizens was underlined by this poll, because for the first time a clear majority—62 percent—said they would prefer Chinese sovereignty to any alternative.

17. Dimbleby (in *The Last Governor*, p. 430) quotes the valedictory comment of the publisher Jimmy Lai, whose papers are almost unique in Hong Kong in crusading for democracy: "It is a shame to have your country colonised, but I have never had this sense of shame, because I have been a free man living in this colony. . . . So long, the British. May God bless you."

18. For a comprehensive and subtle history reflecting, if not in thrall to, post-colonial analyses, see Sugata Bose and Ayesha Jalal, *Modern South Asia: History, Culture, Political Economy* (Delhi: Oxford University Press, 1997). Auden's poem is quoted in Chapter 16.

stated that Hong Kong history texts have to be revised. Though education is supposedly not a matter for the central government under the Basic Law, the new chief executive, C. H. Tung, has confirmed that there would be a need to rewrite the sections on the colonial past.

4

- - - - -

THE CELEBRATION IN Beijing of the reversion of Hong Kong was long planned and efficiently organized. Soon after their fifteenth Party congress this month, the Chinese authorities, if they have not started already, will surely begin planning the celebration of the fiftieth anniversary of the creation of the People's Republic on October 1, 1999. It is crucial for China's Communist leaders that the party-state they created—and major events in the life of the state like the reversion of Hong Kong—should seem all-important to its citizens. India's politicians, on the other hand, are neither appointed nor given legitimacy by the state; they emerge from their party and their community. Faced with the fiftieth anniversary of Independence, the coalition government in New Delhi was so preoccupied with ensuring its own survival that its leaders could hardly focus on a date when they might no longer be in power.

The coalition is still shaky. After the 1996 election, when the Congress government fell, the right-wing Hindu, chauvinist Bharatiya Janata Party (BJP), despite having become the largest party, could not get parliamentary backing for its government. A coalition of thirteen small, mainly regional parties opposed to the BJP came to power, and was maintained in office by the Congress's decision to give it general support. However, the first coalition premier, H. D. Deve Gowda, was toppled in April this year by the Congress Party leader, Sitaram Kesri. And while the coalition government has stayed in office under a new leader, Inder Gujral, Delhi political observers believe that Kesri will withdraw support and force an election in about a year when he anticipates Congress will stand higher in the public opinion polls. But neither they nor their democratic system were threatened by a low-key approach to the golden jubilee.

In both Hong Kong and Delhi the official ceremonies I attended were hard going. The open-air British farewell in Hong Kong took place in an unceasing downpour. Many were sad, all seemed miserable. In New Delhi, at the "stroke of the midnight hour" on August 14, Nehru's speech about India awakening to "life and freedom" to keep its "tryst with destiny" was replayed in the Central Hall of Parliament, and President Narayanan, the first untouchable to become head of state, inveighed against corruption, which he said was "corroding the vitals of our politics and our society."[19]

---

19. In a sad sign of diminishing British expertise on India, an editorial in *The Times* ("Light in dark places," August 18, 1997, p. 19) referred to the prime minister rather than the president as the untouchable.

Everyone understood what he meant. In a jubilee poll, corruption was rated as the greatest national evil, far above unemployment or inflation. Corruption permeates Indian life: politicians buy votes from citizens (though an unusually determined election commissioner cracked down on this practice in the 1996 election). Companies buy favors and licenses to do business from politicians and bureaucrats (though the hope is that freeing the economy from state control will lessen such bribery). Citizens pay "facilitation fees" to the police and petty officials to get access to services. "Even the wretched homeless in some cities have to pay for the right to sleep on the sidewalks," according to Shashi Tharoor in *India: From Midnight to the Millennium*.[20]

The courtesy displayed to Mountbatten fifty years earlier was recaptured by the presence on the dais of Betty Boothroyd, the Speaker of the House of Commons.[21] Outside, we milled around searching desperately for our drivers among hundreds of identical white Indian-made Ambassador cars, still modeled on the 1956 Morris Oxford, hoping for a few hours' sleep before our next tryst with an early-morning speech by the prime minister. This took place at the mid-seventeenth-century Moghul Red Fort in Old Delhi, one of the great

---

20. Arcade, 1997, pp. 254–269.

21. Nehru's attentiveness to Mountbatten and Britain's sensitivities at the time of Independence was detailed by Ajit Bhattacharjea, "The British tilt," *Outlook*, August 13, 1997. It hardly needs be said that correctness rather than sensitivity characterized the Hong Kong handover.

architectural masterpieces commissioned by the Emperor Shah Jahan when he moved his capital from Agra and built the city of Old Delhi.

In Hong Kong, one had to go deep into tourist back alleys to find handover kitsch, a few crude T-shirts; the most common logo visible on Hong Kong citizens' chests was "DKNY." As the rising emigration figures have shown, Hong Kong Chinese are uncertain about their future under Beijing and presumably were not sure whether they had much to celebrate.[22] In New Delhi, at the last minute, the government urged citizens to rush out and buy Indian flags, lifting the normal legal ban on the flag being flown except officially. But Indians were gloomy about the recent downturn in the economy, the violence and fissiparous tendencies spawned by intercaste and communal tensions, and the increasingly criminal character not merely of state assemblies but even of the national parliament, where one estimate is that 100 out of the 535 members of the lower house have criminal records, for crimes such as bribery, rape, and attempted murder.[23] Indians have an overdeveloped capacity for devastating self-criticism

---

22. Emigration averaged about 20,000 in the 1980s until 1987, when it jumped to 30,000, perhaps because of the dismissal of the "liberal" Party general secretary, Hu Yaobang, that January. After Tiananmen there was another jump, and through 1994 the annual figure was regularly 60,000 or over, except in 1993 when it was 53,000. See Ronald Skeldon, editor, *Emigration from Hong Kong: Tendencies and Impacts* (Hong Kong: Chinese University Press, 1995), p. 57.

23. See Hiranmay Karlekar, "The growth of violence has been phenomenal," *The Times of India*, July 31, 1997; the estimate of criminal politicians is given in Tharoor, *India*, p. 266.

and this came out in the many series of articles published during the anniversary, e.g., in *The Times of India*. A popular account of recent travels in small-town India by Pankaj Mishra made it seem as if the previous fifty years had succeeded only in transforming country and people for the worse, with the author wondering "if much of urban India wasn't simply a horrible mistake."[24] The "real India," Mishra writes, is

> broken road, the wandering cows, the open gutter, the low ramshackle shops, the ground littered with garbage, the pressing crowd, the dust.

And the people are no better. The state of Bihar, the land of Buddha, is where

> ... medical colleges sell degrees and doctors pull out transfusion tubes from the veins of their patients when they go on strike, where private caste armies regularly massacre Harijans [untouchables] in droves, where murderers and rapists become legislators through large-scale "booth-capturing"....

---

24. See Pankaj Mishra, *Butter Chicken in Ludhiana: Travels in Small Town India* (Penguin India, 1995), pp. 12, 93, 253. For attempts to provide a more balanced view, see Pran Chopra, "The success side of India," in *The Hindu*, August 5 and 6, 1997. See also Salman Rushdie and Elizabeth West, editors, *Mirrorwork: 50 Years of Indian Writing, 1947–1997* (Henry Holt, 1997), a celebration of Indian writing in English; and Shashi Tharoor's passionate but often agonized avowal of love for his motherland in *India*.

Aged veterans of the struggle against the British expressed their disillusionment to journalists about what had been achieved since 1947 after all their sacrifices.

5

- - - - -

FOR A CHILD of the Raj, it is tempting to believe that the special qualities of both ex-colonies must have something to do with their British legacies: the use of English, for Hong Kong as a bridge to international finance and trade, for India as a link within a polyglot state with eighteen official languages; the rule of law and a well-developed legal structure to protect the citizen and provide a workable market for businessmen; a highly trained and efficient civil service and a relatively uncorrupt police force; and a free press. In the case of India, politicians absorbed the British parliamentary model of democracy and began to practice it in a limited way under the Raj; in Hong Kong, the British stimulated the hunger for one which was introduced too late. Some South Asian historians acknowledge this,[25] and perhaps Hong Kong historians—after understandably excoriating

---

25. See, for example, Ahmed, *Jinnah, Pakistan and Islamic Identity*, pp. 116–117. The most ubiquitous legacy of the British empire is, however, the pipe band.

the Opium War and the subsequent British imperialist ventures that led to the formation of the colony—eventually will too.

173

But the impact of the two-hundred-year engagement of Britain with the rich and complex society of India cannot be described by a complacent list of inherited institutions. Indeed, ever since India's domestic troubles in the 1970s, when Mrs. Gandhi declared martial law, radical Indian historians have been seeking the roots of their discontent in the colonial era.[26] They have had important insights; but their approach and some findings have justifiably been questioned. A widely acclaimed study, for example, depicts a pre-colonial period in which an ecological balance was maintained by a caste system largely without conflict. The arrival of the British, it is argued, disrupted this relatively successful traditional culture by emphasizing production for the market over subsistence, undermining cooperation within communities, and by encouraging the unrestrained use of resources, especially forests. This picture is disputed by Delhi University economist Bina Agarwal, partly on factual grounds, partly because it tends to glorify a traditional social system that was infused with unequal gender relations.[27]

Still, the pros and cons of the British legacy are less

---

26. They call their general approach "subaltern studies." See Guha, *A Subaltern Studies Reader*, especially the introduction.

27. The claims about caste and ecological balance, and the effects of the British, are to be found in Madhav Gadgil and Ramachandra Guha, *This Fissured Land: An Ecological History of India* (University of California Press, 1992), pp. 113–116. For critiques of subaltern studies, see C.A. Bayly

important for outsiders with an affection for India than the ongoing commitment to parliamentary democracy and the rule of law, though these are marred by glaring political problems and social failures. As an American observer put it, "galloping normlessness" characterizes Indian politics. The statistics on social conditions remain dismaying. Infant malnutrition is worse than in sub-Saharan Africa. The ineffectiveness of family planning means that a population that was 350 million in 1947 is now 950 million, will be about 1,580 million in another fifty years, and may not become stabilized for another hundred years. The percentage of people below the poverty line has declined from over 55 percent when the British left, but it is still well over a third of the much larger population. The neglect of primary health care, especially for women, is attested to by the infant mortality rate of 75 per 1,000, as compared with 31 in China, 41 in Egypt, and 53 in Indonesia, and with a world rate of 63. There is still desperate poverty and not just in Calcutta.[28]

A particularly sad failure is suggested by the fact that no more than 52 percent of the population is literate—as compared with a world rate of 76 percent—

---

in *Empires and Information: Intelligence Gathering and Social Communication in India, 1780–1870* (Cambridge University Press, 1996), p. 368, and Sumit Sarkar, *Writing Social History* (New Delhi: Oxford University Press, 1997), pp. 82–108.

28. See Amartya Sen, "How India has fared," *Frontline*, August 22, 1997. It is worth pointing out, in view of the immense publicity that has attended Mother Teresa's good works in Calcutta and her funeral there, that an extraordinary number and range of Indian private institutions try to substitute for government in providing welfare not only in Calcutta but in many other cities and villages.

with an Indian female rate of only 36 percent. Though 80 percent of Indian children now start primary school, the failure to spread primary education is attested by the fact that only 40.8 percent of Indians are literate at age fifteen as compared with 90 percent of South Koreans, 72.6 percent of Chinese, and 57.3 percent of Ugandans.[29] There were plausible grounds for the pessimism felt by many Indians as they looked back over five decades.

But India's leaders should be credited for trying to deal with fundamental cleavages in Indian society. The Indian caste system has been around for millennia; the Muslim invasions started over a thousand years ago. But the social and communal problems begotten by that history were confronted at the outset of Independence, initially through the agony of Partition, and then through rights and safeguards written into the constitution. It abolished untouchability and said that citizens could not be denied access to shops, restaurants, and other public places on grounds of caste and religion.[30] It promised special treatment for the untouchable castes and tribes which it listed in a special

---

29. Jagdish Bhagwati, *India in Transition: Freeing the Economy* (Oxford University Press/Clarendon Press, 1993), p. 48. Resources that might have gone into primary education have been invested in higher education. Taking into account differences in population size, India sends six times as many people to universities as China; see Amartya Sen, "Wrongs and rights in development," *Prospect*, October 1995, p. 30.

30. Contrast this with the American race problem. It is 400 years old. It was finessed at the founding of the United States. After fifty years, the problem had still not even been confronted. By its centenary, the US was emerging from a bloody Civil War and an abortive Reconstruction which failed to lay the problem to rest. Only around the time of the country's two-hundredth

"schedule." In fulfilling these undertakings, the Indian government has reserved 22.5 percent of government jobs and 85 seats in the legislature for members of "scheduled" castes and tribes.

But it is worth emphasizing that attempts to help other backward castes (OBCs), people above the level of untouchability, have caused even more political upheavals than affirmative action for minorities in the US—including the collapse of governments. On August 7, 1990, the then prime minister, V. P. Singh, announced that his government would honor the ten-year-old recommendations of an official commission that 27 percent of all federal government jobs should be reserved for OBCs. In the words of Mr. Singh, all hell broke loose: government buses were burned, trains were attacked, public property was extensively damaged, and some upper-caste youths immolated themselves. His government fell.

Religious tensions have also risen since the bloody violence unleashed in 1992 when the Babri Masjid mosque in Ayodhya was destroyed by Hindus who claimed it had been built on top of an ancient temple to the god Rama. The secularism of the founding fathers is under siege.[31]

anniversary was the US civil rights movement able to demand that the state bring about changes that should have been accomplished by the Civil War.

31. For a discussion of these deeply troubling issues, see Tharoor, *India*, pp. 50–78; for an attempt to provide a new analytical approach with which to understand post-independence ethnic violence, see Stanley Tambiah, *Leveling Crowds: Ethnonationalist Conflicts and Collective Violence in South Asia* (University of California Press, 1996).

Still, acting under far greater pressures than ever constrained the officers of the Raj's Indian Civil Service, Indian politicians and bureaucrats have managed to maintain national unity and a democratic polity. We should remember that in the 1950s, there was speculation that India might fall apart or survive only by totalitarian means,[32] and that in the late 1960s, under Mrs. Gandhi, it was confidently predicted that India had held its last election. The problems remain, but India has held together and the democratic system has taken root among the voters, even if they have an understandable skepticism about what the politicians will actually deliver: 59 percent assert that their vote makes a difference and only 21 percent say the opposite; 69 percent reject the idea that governance would be better without parties and elections, even though 63 percent feel that representatives do not care about the people.[33]

From afar, India's problems look insuperable. The benefit of returning there is to be reminded of the talent, resilience, and determination that abound for tackling them. With economic reform taking hold and the growth rate reaching a healthy 7 percent, India at fifty is making progress, still slowly, always painfully, but with gathering momentum. Hong Kong at year zero is

---

32. The most prominent discussion of these issues was in Selig S. Harrison, *India: The Most Dangerous Decades* (Princeton University Press, 1960).

33. "The maturing of a democracy," *India Today*, August 31, 1996, p. 41. In a less detailed poll a year later, however, 53 percent voted against the "government's policy based on caste"; *India Today*, August 18, 1997, p. 49.

of course enviably better off and always hustling. Its citizens have been promised their own "system" for fifty years. But will Hong Kong at fifty be the mature democracy India is today? Only if China is too.

SEPTEMBER 25, 1997

Hilary
Mantel

- - - - -

STATES
OF
EMERGENCY

"UN ROMAN EST UN MIROIR..." Stendhal said. "A novel is a mirror which passes over a highway. Sometimes it reflects to your eyes the blue of the skies, at others the churned-up mud of the road." Of course, not all novelists choose to carry mirrors of perfect clarity. Some travel with just a wicked sliver of glass, some strut along with a gleeful grin and a distorting mirror; others respectfully support a windowpane through which little is seen but the author's own face. But when Rohinton Mistry published his first novel, *Such a Long Journey* (1991), we seemed to have found an author who would carry a mirror for us down the dusty highways of India, through the jostling Bombay streets, behind compound walls and into the huts and houses where the millions sit, reinventing themselves, constantly reciting the stories of their own lives and times. His documentary realism won praise. The writing seemed a world away from Rushdie's aggressive surrealism and linguistic tricks. The prose was plain, the tone often jaunty. Human decency came shining through.

Such a Long Journey was shortlisted for the Booker Prize and won the Governor General's Award in Canada. It was a fluent and involving chronicle of the family and neighborhood life of a Parsi called Gustad Noble, a likable man perpetually baffled by what destiny threw at him. It was not unflawed; there was some perfunctory plotting, a strain of sentimentality. Its great virtue was that it kept background and foreground in perspective. The perplexities and concerns of small people, the citizens of Bombay in the early 1970s, were set against a threatening international situation. Their everyday aspirations and disappointments entertained us, while India and Pakistan moved toward war. In his new novel, *A Fine Balance*,[1] Mistry carries us on to 1975, when Indira Gandhi declared a State of Emergency and suspended civil liberties.

Here again intimate dramas will be played out against the vast canvas of the subcontinent. But where the first novel began in a gentle, careful miniaturist's manner, reminiscent of R. K. Narayan, the tone here is menacing. You had better believe me, Mistry seems to tell us: brace yourself for what is to come. In his epigraph he quotes Balzac, *Le Père Goriot*:

> "After you have read this story of great misfortunes, you will no doubt dine well.... But rest assured: this tragedy is not fiction. All is true."

The book begins with a railway journey. The train is

---

1. Knopf, 1996.

late. There is a body on the tracks. The passengers are more than usually exasperated: "Why does everybody have to choose the railways tracks only for dying? . . . Murder, suicide, Naxalite-terrorist killing, police-custody death—everything ends up delaying the trains. What is wrong with poison or tall buildings or knives?"

One carriage contains three people with a common destination. Maneck Kohlah is a Parsi student; Ishvar Darji and Omprakash Darji are Hindu tailors, uncle and nephew, respectively forty-seven and seventeen years old. They are new to city life; the two tailors are displaced from a village in the plains, while Maneck is a long journey from his misty northern home in the mountains. It is the exigencies of displacement that bring them together, and to the tiny, shabby city apartment of Dina, a Parsi widow in her early forties. Maneck is to be a paying guest. Repelled by the squalid conditions in his student hostel, he has appealed to his parents for help, and his mother has arranged for him to stay with an old school friend of hers. The tailors are to do piecework for Dina, sewing women's clothing for an export company.

Dina could have expected better than the cramped, penny-pinching, anxious life that she has come to live in middle age. Her father was a doctor, a selfless, hard-driven man who died from snakebite while toiling in one of the fever-ridden villages of the interior. She was twelve years old then, and her mother's nervous collapse left her upbringing in the hands of Nusswan, her twenty-three-year-old brother, already established as a young businessman. Quarrels with

Nusswan brought an early end to her education, but she married—married a man she herself had chosen, in defiance of Nusswan's wishes—and was happy for three years, until her husband was killed in a traffic accident.

Though her brother presses her to join his household, Dina is determined to stay in her flat and to support herself. When the three men come into her life, she is wary of what their companionship may mean—loneliness is what she is used to. Besides, the tailors are uncouth villagers who scratch themselves and cannot use cutlery, and Maneck is so young, and spoiled perhaps?

The evolution of an odd, mutually dependent household is at the center of the book. The characters' halting progress toward each other is described with great sensitivity; it is a tale of pride and prejudice, of simple affection breaking barriers. When the tailors begin to work for Dina they are sleeping on the street. They get a hut in a shantytown and gather a few possessions, but their hut is bulldozed. They are on the streets again, and eventually Dina takes them in, even though she knows that their presence is against the terms of her lease and that her landlord is looking for an excuse to evict her. She is acting against her better judgment, her heart for once ruling her head; reserved, cautious, sometimes shrewish, she is a character to whom Mistry allows great dignity.

Maneck and his family are drawn with quiet sympathy. Wealthy people who lost their lands in 1947 when India and Pakistan separated, they have built up a general store, but trade is failing now, and they feel their only son should get professional qualifications. They do not want to send him away; he does not want to go. But parents and child are blind to each other's signals, too proud to confess their need of each other. It is a quiet, small-scale, low-key tragedy. Maneck feels his family has rejected him. A shy, fastidious, depressive boy, he takes some comfort in his unlikely friendship with Om, the childlike, boisterous young tailor. Meanwhile Ishvar impresses Dina with his quiet self-sufficiency, his ability to absorb life's worst blows. Early in the book there is a heavy hint of something grim in the tailors' past. The narrative loops back to the time of Om's grandfather, and we learn what it is.

The tailors' family belongs to the caste of leather-workers. Their work is highly unpleasant, their resources scanty. Om's grandfather commits the crime of wishing to better himself. He sends his two sons, Ishvar and Narayan, to the nearest small town, where they are apprenticed to his Muslim friend Ashraf, a tailor. It is a huge rebellion—against tradition, against fate.

When they grow up, Ishvar stays in town as Ashraf's assistant. Narayan goes back to the village, sets up shop, and makes a point of sewing for customers of all castes. He becomes successful, marries, builds a big house for himself, his parents, and his business. He has a son, Om, and two daughters. The author has already introduced us to the miseries of the caste system, the repression, violence, and humiliation suffered by the village people at the hands of landlords and their agents. We know that Narayan is courting disaster.

This is an intensely angry book, a political novel that

pulls no punches. Mistry loathes the Congress Party,
which has held power in India for all but four of the
forty-nine years since Independence. He sees the party
as the purveyor of empty promises of amelioration,
the propagator of progressive social legislation that is
passed but never enforced. There is a scathing set-piece
description of Indira Gandhi addressing a rally; it cap-
tures all the Prime Minister's self-deluding compla-
cency, all the self-serving hypocrisy of her supporters. It
is as effective a demolition job as a novelist can do.

Yet when Mistry approaches the most harrowing
event of his book, his tone is deceptively cool, as if
indignation were bleached out, as if the facts spoke for
themselves.

An election is scheduled—the date is not given, but
we are in the early 1970s.

> On election day the eligible voters in the village
> lined up outside the polling station. As usual,
> Thakur Dharamsi [the local magnate] took
> charge of the voting process. His system, with the
> support of the other landlords, had been working
> flawlessly for years.
>
> The election officer was presented with gifts
> and led away to enjoy the day with food and
> drink. The doors opened and the voters filed
> through. "Put out your fingers," said the atten-
> dant monitoring the queue.
>
> The voters complied. The clerk at the desk un-
> capped a little bottle and marked each extended fin-
> ger with indelible black ink, to prevent cheating.

"Now put your thumbprints over here," said the clerk.

They placed their thumbprints on the register to say they had voted, and departed.

Then the blank ballots were filled in by the landlords' men.

Two years on there is another election. Narayan decides he will no longer take part in the farce. He goes to the polling booth and tries to register a genuine vote. Two neighbors back him up. When we learn what happens next we understand why Mistry's approach has been so deceptively calm. The three men are picked up by Thakur's men and taken to his farm. They are suspended upside down and flogged, through the length of a day. Burning coals are held against their genitals and forced into their mouths. In the evening they are hanged. The corpses are displayed in the village square.

And while the torture goes on, Thakur's little grandchildren are shut up indoors. Play with your nice new train set, he urges them, smiling. For the first time in the book we catch the whiff of the concentration camp; a mild paterfamilias steps out of his front door to exercise the rabid dog inside him. We catch the same whiff in the horrifying description of a work camp where Om and his uncle toil when they are picked up on the streets, along with beggars and pavement dwellers. The Nazi stench is overpowering when Dina's brother Nusswan, reflecting on his country's plight, advocates "a free meal containing arsenic or cyanide" for the "two hundred million people surplus to requirements."

It is not that, by this point in the book, Nusswan has become a vicious caricature. What we learn of Nusswan's bullying tactics within his family does not lead us to admire him, but he is not inherently a bad man, and Mistry makes us reflect how often such bigotry stains the lips of otherwise kindly, dutiful individuals. In the face of the world's beauty, in the face of the self-evident fact of altruism, how can atrocious conduct occur, how can hideous beliefs survive? The question is age-old, and Mistry has no answers, but it is evident from the seriousness and weight of the present book that he believes that novelists should go on asking, and asking.

After the death of Narayan and his two nameless supporters there is worse to come. The landlords' men rampage through the village. They carry Narayan's mutilated body to his house and display it to his wife. They then tie up Narayan's wife, his little daughters, and his parents, and set fire to the hut. Om and Ishvar, safe in town, are the only survivors of their family.

This atrocity, which is placed by the author about a quarter of the way through the narrative, stretches its black shadow over the whole book. Mistry's very success in harrowing the reader will create a problem for him. We cannot read the next 450 pages without some alleviation, some lightening of the tone; yet how does an author achieve this, when he has so much more in store for his characters? The horrors of the forced sterilization program—with its potential not only for blood poisoning but for the settling of old scores—will reduce the patient Ishvar to a beggar with amputated legs, will reduce his spirited nephew to a puffy eunuch pulling his uncle on a wheeled platform. In the face of such horrifying material, the gentle humor of Mistry's earlier book cannot help the reader along, and his occasional attempts at levity become an irritating tic. A reader can perhaps bear an escalation of disaster and misery; what is almost unbearable is the cyclical pattern of disaster in which Mistry has trapped his creations. Every time life improves a little, every time they raise their low expectations a notch, disaster strikes. In the end one feels controlled, as if by a bad god. This, no doubt, is part of Mistry's intent.

By the closing stages of the book, no veil of irony is drawn over authorial manipulation. Shankar the beggar, known as "Worm," is the most pathetic of all Mistry's creations. With no legs and deformed arms, he pushes himself around on a wheeled platform like the one on which Ishvar will end his days. He is given "protection" and guaranteed his pitch by the Beggarmaster, who takes a share of the offerings made to him—and who turns out to be his half brother. Shankar keeps, for comfort, some tails of human hair; absurdly, he is accused of the murder of their original owners. Escaping from an angry crowd, he is crushed by a bus. His grotesque funeral procession is attacked by riot police, who believe the participants to be politically inspired mummers "indulging in street theatre" and the corpse to be a "symbolic dummy."

Mistry here is making a dangerously destructive comment on his own technique. Like the Beggarmaster, the author is keen on getting a good return from Shankar. He has used him to tease and torment our most tender sensibilities; then, through a strenuous sequence of plot developments, we are primed for him to meet a gruesome end. It is a miscalculation; we see that Mistry himself has made a "symbolic dummy" of the weakest and most vulnerable of all his creations. One reviewer has already compared Mistry to Dickens, and it is plain that his energy and his panoramic ambition are on the same scale. It may be, though, that he has one of Dickens's less-applauded traits; when his characters fall below a certain income level, he stereotypes them. It may be true that "the rich are different," but it does not follow that the very poor are all the same. The novelist who writes in the realist tradition must take the trouble to grow his characters. Poor Worm can hardly evolve; a theatrical end is dealt out to him. He is ours to look at; he is not ours to feel with.

Images—of fate, of time, of destiny—cluster like flies around the narratives' death throes. "The lives of the poor were rich in symbols," Dina reflects—and again Mistry is playing with fire, for his reader may retort that all our lives are rich in symbols when we have such a determined, schematic author on our trail. The book's great questions are not drawn together gently, but hauled weightily into the foreground. Time and fate are variously a quilt, a devouring lizard, a chess grandmaster who can never be checkmated. And yet it is the most naive images, simple and melancholy, that stay with the reader.

"If time were a bolt of cloth," said Om, "I would cut out all the bad parts. Snip out the scary nights and stitch together the good parts, to make time bearable. Then I could wear it like a coat, always live happily."

Calling attention to the nature of his own work, Mistry makes his characters reflect on the art and craft of story-making. "Perhaps the very act of telling created a natural design. Perhaps it was a knack that humans had, for cleaning up their untidy existences—a hidden survival weapon, like antibodies in the bloodstream."

Mistry's work does not need this authorial endorsement. Few readers who have weathered the six hundred pages will need to be told that this is a serious and important book, that it is the product of high intelligence and passionate conviction. It is remarkable, in a narrative so overdetermined, that the four major characters breathe and flourish as individuals. The details of their daily lives, the nuances of their feelings, are presented to us respectfully. The final pages are coarser—perhaps the book should have been longer? The "fine balance" of which one character speaks—the balance between hope and despair—is exquisitely difficult to maintain. The placing of an incident, the timing of a passage, are crucial; the urgent, almost brutal energy which Mistry brings to his project tips us to the side of despair.

In the end, Mistry chooses to divide the fates of his four companions. Maneck commits suicide, though he is young, healthy, educated—he has, so to speak, nothing to commit suicide about. The less fortunate face life with more courage. Dina ends as a drudge in her brother's kitchen, secretly feeding the tailors-turned-beggars every afternoon, while they in turn nourish her with their warmth and their wit. Is Mistry feeding us an old line—telling us, rightly or wrongly, that what is inside a human being counts for more than external circumstance? We have been made witness to events that leave a stain on the soul; the resilience of spirit with which the tailors face their final degradation seems admirable, but slightly beside the point.

Perhaps the key lies in one of the many conversations that take place on trains. Maneck meets a man who used to be a proofreader for *The Times of India*— a man who for twenty-four years saw a record of his country's daily griefs and disasters pass before his eyes. Would it be effective, Maneck wonders, if everybody in India got angry? Might that force the politicians to change their ways? Sometimes, says the proofreader, it is better to suppress anger. "Just try to imagine six hundred million raging, howling, sobbing humans.... Would the mountains explode? What about rivers, would the tears from twelve hundred million eyes cause them to rise and flood?"

This experienced man preaches not quiescence but containment. Yet one day, he admits, the very words on the page rebelled. The letters pitched and tossed and mutinied. He could not read. The paper beneath his hand became a stormy sea. His eyes watered, his head swam; he collapsed. He had developed, he later discovered, a violent allergy to printer's ink. He had lived by the word and almost perished by it. He had explored its limits, and his own.

This is what Rohinton Mistry has done. He has lived

in Canada for some years, which is perhaps as well, for this book will not make him popular in his native country. At the time of writing, the Congress Party has been humiliated in a general election, and the Hindu nationalists have formed a minority government. Their Bharatiya Janata Party is widely regarded as traditionalist if not retrogressive, inimical to the lower castes and to the Muslim population. Perhaps Mistry is right and—as the odious phrase has it—what goes around, comes around.

Huge, ambitious novels tend to succumb to platitudes in the end. Unless the author is a genius, they are sucked into cliché by their aspirations to universality. This is one of Mistry's problems. Another problem runs deeper. The novel is an optimistic form. It offers its characters some freedom, within their created nature, and an afterlife in the imagination of readers. But Mistry's characters—even those who are not Hindu—are caught in a vast, predetermined, prepatterned design, which the author embroiders fiercely, glibly. The narrative is closely sewn and makes effective patterns. Design is necessary, but the author should distinguish his own needs from those of the characters and those of the reader; a given fate is not necessarily one to which the characters should be resigned. Here they have no choice or hope. They loiter forever on street corners, hoping to catch the bus but knowing it is likely that when it comes it will mow them down; the driver's name is Mistry, and within his six hundred pages he will crush them all.

Pankaj
Mishra

- - - - -

E D M U N D   W I L S O N

I N

B E N A R E S

1

I SPENT FOUR months in Benares in the winter of 1988. I was twenty years old, with no clear idea of my future, or indeed much of anything else. After three idle, bookish years at a provincial university in a decaying old provincial town, I had developed an aversion to the world of careers and jobs which, having no money, I was destined to join. In Benares, the holiest city of the Hindus, where people come either to ritually dissolve their accumulated "sins" in the Ganges, or simply to die and achieve liberation from the cycle of rebirths—in Benares, with a tiny allowance, I sought nothing more than a continuation of the life I had led as an undergraduate.

I lived in the old quarter, in a half-derelict house owned by a Brahmin musician, a tiny, frail, courteous old man. Panditji had long ago cut himself off from the larger world, and lay sunk all day long in an opium-induced daze, from which he roused himself punctually at six in the evening to give sitar lessons to German and American students. It was how he maintained his expensive habit, and also staved off penury. His estranged, asthmatic wife lived on the floor above his—she claimed to have not gone downstairs for fifteen years—and spent most of her time in a windowless kitchen full of smoke from the dung-paved hearth, conversing in a low voice with her faithful family retainer of over fifty years. The retainer, a small, reticent man in pleated khaki shorts, hinted, in that gloomy setting, at better days in the past, even a kind of feudal grandeur.

The house I lived in, the melancholy presence of Panditji and his wife, were part of the world of old Benares that was still intact in the late Eighties, and of which the chess games in the alleys, the all-night concerts in temples, the dancing girls at elaborately formal weddings, the gently decadent pleasures of betel leaves and opium formed an essential component. In less than two years, most of this solid-seeming world was to vanish into thin air. The old city was to be scarred by a rash of fast-food outlets, video-game parlors, and boutiques, the most garish symbols of the entrepreneurial energies unleashed by the liberalization of the Indian economy, which would transform Benares in the way they had transformed other sleepy small towns across India.

But I didn't know this then, and I did not listen too closely when Panditji's wife reminisced about the Benares she had known as a young woman, when she told me about the time her husband came to her family home as a starving student, when she described to me the honors bestowed on her father by the Maharajah of Benares. I was even less attentive when she complained to me about her son and his wife, more particularly the latter, who, though Brahmin, had, in her opinion, the greedy, grasping ways of the merchant castes.

I didn't pay much attention to the lives around me. I was especially indifferent to the wide-eyed Europeans drifting about on the old ghats, each attached to an ash-smeared Guru. I was deep into my own world, and, though I squirmed at the word and the kinds of abject dependence it suggested, I had found my own Guru, long dead, but, to me, more real than anyone I knew the winter I spent slowly making my way through his books.

On an earlier visit to the library at Benares Hindu University, idly browsing through the stacks, I had noticed a book called *The American Earthquake*. I read a few pages at random, standing in a dark corridor between overloaded, dusty shelves. It seemed interesting; I made a mental note to look it up on my next trip to the library. Months passed. By then I had moved to Benares, and one day while looking for something else in the same part of the stacks, I came across the book again. I took it to the reading room this time. An hour into it, I began to look at the long list under the heading "Other books by Edmund Wilson." Later that afternoon, I went back to the stacks, where they all were, dust-laden, termite-infested, but beautifully, miraculously, present: *The Shores of Light, Classics and Commercials, The Bit Between My Teeth, The Wound and the Bow, Europe Without Baedeker, A Window on Russia, A Piece of My Mind. . . .*

It was miraculous because this was no ordinary library. Wilson's books weren't easily accessible. I had always lived in small towns where libraries and bookshops were few and far between, and did not stock anything except a few standard texts of English literature: Austen, Dickens, Kipling, Thackeray. My semicolonial education had made me spend much of my time on minor Victorian and Edwardian writers. Some diversity was provided by writers in Hindi and the Russians, which you could buy cheaply at Communist bookstores. As for the rest, I read randomly, whatever I could find, and with the furious intensity of a small-town boy to whom books are the sole means of communicating with, and understanding, the larger world.

I had realized early on that being passionate about literature wasn't enough. You had to be resourceful; you had to be perpetually on the hunt for books. And so I was, at libraries and bookshops, at other people's houses, in letters to relatives in the West, and, most fruitfully, at the local paper recycler, where I once bought a tattered old paperback of Heinrich Mann's *Man of Straw*, which I—such were the gaps in my knowledge—dutifully read, and made notes about, without knowing anything about his more famous and distinguished brother. Among this disconnected reading, I had certain preferences, a few strong likes and dislikes, but they did not add up to coherent standards of judgment. I knew little of the social and historical underpinnings to the books I read; I had only a fleeting sense of the artistry and skill to which certain novels owed their greatness.

I had problems, too, with those books of Edmund Wilson I had found at the library, some of which I read in part that winter, others from cover to cover. They constantly referred to other books I hadn't heard of; many of them were collections of reviews of books I could not possibly read at the time. Proust, Joyce, Hemingway, Waugh, yes; Malraux and Silone, probably; but where in India could one find John Dos Passos? Wilson's books also assumed a basic knowledge of politics and history I did not have. They were a struggle for me, and the ignorance I felt before them was a secret source of shame, but it was also a better stimulus to the effort Wilson's books demanded than mere intellectual curiosity.

I was never to cease feeling this ignorance, but I also had a sense as I groped my way through his work that all those unread books and unknown writers were coming to me filtered through an extraordinarily cohesive sensibility. Over the next few months, it became clear to me that his powers of summary and explication were often worth more attention than the books and writers that were his subject. There was also a certain idea that his lucid prose and confident judgments suggested, and that, at first, I found so attractive about him: the idea of a man wholly devoted to reading and thinking and writing. I thought of him at work in his various residences—Provincetown, Talcottville, Cambridge, Wellfleet—and these resonant names became attached in my imagination to a promise of wisdom and serenity.

The library where I had found Wilson's books had, along with the university, come out of an old, and now vanished, impulse, the desire among Hindu reformists in the freedom movement to create indigenous centers of education and culture. The fundamental idea was to train young Hindu men for the modern world; and, like many other idealisms of the freedom movement, it hadn't survived long in the chaos of independent India, where even the right to education came to be fiercely fought over under the banner of specific castes, religions, regions, and communities.

Sectarian tensions were particularly intense in North India, especially here in Uttar Pradesh, the province with the greatest population and second highest poverty rate in the country, where caste and political rivalries spread to the local universities. The main political parties,[1] eager to enlist the large student vote in their favor, had begun to put money into elections to the student unions. Politically ambitious students would organize themselves by caste—the Brahmin, the Thakur (the so-called warrior caste), the Backward, and the Scheduled (the government's euphemism for former untouchables). The tensions were so great that academic sessions were frequently interrupted by student strikes; arson, kidnapping, and murder among students became common features of campus life.

Miraculously, the library at Benares had remained well stocked. Subscriptions to foreign magazines had been renewed on time: you could find complete volumes of the TLS, *Partisan Review*, and *The New York Review of Books* from the 1960s in the stacks.

---

1. For many years Benares was a stronghold of left-wing parties. In recent elections, however, the BJP candidate has won.

Catalogues of university presses had been dutifully
scrutinized by the library staff; the books, as though
through some secluded channel untouched by the surrounding disorder, had kept flowing in.

The library was housed in an impressively large
building in the style known as Hindu-Saracenic, whose
attractive pastiche of Hindu and Victorian Gothic
architecture had been prompted by the same Indian
modernist aspirations that had created the university.
But now chaos reigned in almost every department:
few books were to be found in their right places; the
card catalog was in complete disarray. In the reading
room, students of a distinctly criminal appearance
smoked foul-smelling cigarettes and noisily played
cards. Some of them chose to take their siestas on long
desks; bored young women spent hours scratching
their initials on table tops.

It was hardly a congenial place for long hours of
reading, but since I wasn't enrolled as a student at the
university, I could not take books out of the library. I
was, however, allowed to sit in the reading room, and I
was there almost every day from the time it opened in
the morning. Since I had little money, I walked the four
miles to the library from my house. For lunch I had an
omelette at a fly-infested stall outside the library, and
then hurried back after a glass of sticky-sweet tea
which effectively killed all hunger for the next few
hours. In the evening, I would walk home along the
river and sit until after dark on the ghats, among a
mixed company of touts and drug-pushers; washermen
gathering clothes that had rested on the stone steps all

afternoon, white and sparkling in the sun; groups of children playing hopscotch on the chalk-marked stone floor; a few late bathers, dressing and undressing under tattered beach umbrellas; and the groups of old men, silently gazing at the darkening river.

Many of my days in Benares were spent in this way, and when I think of them they seem serenely uneventful. But what I remember best now are not so much the clear blue skies and magically still afternoons, glimpsed from my window-side perch at the library, as the peculiar factors that constantly threatened to undo that serenity. For a radically different world existed barely a few hundred meters from where I sat, reading about Santayana.

The university in those days was the scene of intense battles between students and the police. Anything could provoke them: a student who was not readmitted after being expelled, an exam that a professor refused to postpone. A peculiar frenzy periodically overtook the two sides when the students rampaged through the campus, smashing furniture and windowpanes left unbroken from their last eruption of rage. Challenged by the police, they retreated to the sanctuary of their hostels and fired pistols at the baton-charging constables. In retaliation, the policemen often invaded the hostels, broke into locked rooms, dragged out their pleading, wailing occupants, and proceeded to beat them.

I once saw one of their victims, minutes after the police had left, coughing blood and broken teeth, his clothes torn, the baton marks on his exposed arms rapidly turning blue. Another time I saw a policeman with half of the flesh and bones on his back gouged out by a locally made hand grenade. Anxious colleagues watched helplessly from behind their wire mesh shields as he tottered and collapsed on the ground. Terrified bystanders like myself threw themselves to the ground in a defensive reflex we'd seen in action movies. The grenade thrower—a scrawny boy in a big-collared shirt and tight polyester pants who, I learned later, had targeted the policeman after being tortured by him in custody—stood watching on the cobblestone road, fascinated by his handiwork.

Such violence, extreme though it seemed, wasn't new to the university, which had long been witness to bloodier battles between student wings of Communist and Hindu nationalist organizations. These two groups tended to be allied with different ends of the caste system: the lower castes tended to be Communist; the upper castes tended to be Hindu nationalist. But frequently now, the violence came for no ideological reason, with no connections to a cause or movement. It erupted spontaneously, fueled only by the sense of despair and hopelessness that permanently hung over North Indian universities in the 1980s. It was part of a larger crisis caused by the collapse of many Indian institutions, the increasingly close alliance between crime and politics, and the growth of state-organized corruption—processes that had been speeded up during Mrs. Gandhi's "Emergency" in the mid-Seventies.

For students poised to enter this world, the choices were harsh—and it didn't matter what caste you belonged to; poverty was evenly distributed across caste divisions in this region. Most of the people I knew were deeply cynical in their attitude toward their future. You could work toward becoming a member of either the state or national legislature and siphon off government funds earmarked for literacy and population-control projects; if nothing worked out, you could aspire, at the other end of the scale, to be a lowly telephone mechanic and make money by selling illegal telephone connections.

Most of the students in this traditionally backward region of India came from feudal or semirural families, and aspired to join the Civil Service, a colonial invention which in independent India continued to offer the easiest and quickest route to political power and affluence. But there were fewer and fewer recruitments made to the Civil Service from North India, where the decline in standards, as well as the cheap availability, of higher education had made it possible for millions to acquire university degrees while they had less and less prospect of employment. Bribery and nepotism had a major part in the disbursement of the jobs in the minor government services. Students from the lately impoverished upper castes suffered most in this respect: if poverty wasn't enough, they were further disadvantaged by the large quotas for lower-caste candidates in government jobs.

The quotas, first created by Nehru's government in the early 1950s and meant as a temporary measure, were expanded and used by successive governments as an electoral ploy to attract lower-caste votes. The upper-caste students found themselves making the dif-

ficult adjustments to urban life only to confront the
prospect of being sent back to the oblivion they had
emerged from; and their sense of blocked futures,
which they acquired early in their time at the university, was to reach a tragic culmination in 1990 in the
spate of self-immolations following the central government's decision to provide even larger quotas in federal
jobs for applicants from lower castes.

My own situation was little different from that of
the people around me. I had recently spent three years
at the nearby provincial university at Allahabad, where
I was in even closer, more unsettling, proximity to the
desperation I saw in Benares. I was upper-caste myself,
without family wealth, and roughly in the same position as my father had been in freshly independent India
when the land reform act of 1951—another of Nehru's
attempts at social equality, it was meant to turn
exploited tenants into landholders—reduced his once
well-to-do Brahmin family to penury. My mother's
family had suffered a similar setback. Like many others
in my family who laboriously worked their way into
the middle classes, I had to make my own way in the
world. Looking back, I can see my compulsive pursuit
of books, and the calm and order it suggests, contrasting so jarringly with the rage and desperation around
me, as my way of putting off a grimly foreclosed future.

So, during my months in Benares, I was able to live
at a slight tangent to the chaos of the university. And I
was able to do this, I now see, partly because of Rajesh.

2

- - - - -

I GOT TO know Rajesh early in my stay at Benares. A tall, wiry, good-looking man in his mid-twenties, he had continued to live in Benares after he had finished his studies at the university. He was eccentric and moody: he would start reciting Urdu poetry one moment and then denounce its decadence the next, and start enumerating the virtues of the farming life. "All these wine drinkers with broken hearts," he would say. "You can't compare them to simple peasants who do more for humanity." He used to say he would rather be a farmer than join government service and do the bidding of corrupt politicians. On other occasions, he would tell me about the good works honest civil servants in India could achieve, and how he himself aspired to be one of them. There was also an unexpected mystical side to him. I once saw him standing on the ghats gesturing toward the sandy expanses across the river. "That," he was saying to his companion, a slightly terrified young student, "is *sunyata*, the void." "And this," he pointed at the teeming conglomeration of temples and houses behind us, "is *Maya*, illusion. Do you know what our task is? Our task is to live somewhere in between."

He revered Gandhi, and distrusted Nehru, who he said was too "modern" in his outlook; but then he would change his mind and say that Gandhi wasn't "tough" enough. All of these opinions he delivered with a faraway look; they formed part of monologues about the degraded state of contemporary India. "Where are we going?" he would say, dramatically throwing up his hands. "What kind of nation are we becoming?" He loved Faiz, the Pakistani writer whose doom-laden poetry he knew by heart; he was also fond of Wordsworth, whom he had studied as an undergraduate; he showed me a notebook where he had copied down his favorite poems, "The Solitary Reaper" among them. But I could never get him to talk about them. He did not listen much; and he did not like anyone interrupting his monologues. It wasn't easy to be with him.

He had been at the university for eight years when I met him, and at first he appeared another of the countless students who hung around the campus, mechanically accumulating useless degrees, applying for this or that job. I had come to him with an introduction from a mutual friend at my undergraduate university. This friend believed that "studious" people like myself needed powerful "backers" at Benares Hindu University—he used the English words—and that Rajesh was well placed to protect me from local bullies and criminals. Rajesh himself believed so, and was more than happy to take me under his wing. "You are here to study," he told me at our first meeting, "and that's what you should do. Let me know if anyone bothers you and I'll fix the bastard."

Part of his concern for me came from an old, and now slightly melodramatic, reverence for "studious" Brahmins. He was Brahmin himself, but considered himself unequal to what he felt to be the proper dignity of his caste. The feeling was widespread in the region, where the traditional dominance of Brahmins was beginning to collapse in the face of a serious political challenge by assertive lower castes. The decline of Brahmin prestige and authority—which was intimately linked to their diminishing political importance—was symbolized by a famous family of Benares, which was once very close to the Nehru–Gandhi dynasty, and had been pushed into irrelevance by the new, militant kind of low-caste politician. The members of the family still wore their caste marks on their foreheads; they still observed fasts, regularly bathed in the Ganges, were chief guests at temples on holy days, and would not accept food from low-caste people. But it was only this excessive concern about their public image, and an overdeveloped sense of uncleanliness and contamination, that remained of their Brahminness. No crowds of job seekers and flunkeys gathered at their house anymore; the women in the family went around the bazaars unescorted and unrecognized; visiting journalists went elsewhere for good copy.

Rajesh felt the general change of status differently. He fasted religiously, went to offer flowers at the temple of Hanuman, the monkey god, every Tuesday. His regard for Faiz and love for Urdu poetry spoke of an older Brahminical instinct for learning and the arts. But he also gave the impression that none of the old ways or values mattered anymore in a world in which Brahmins were forced to struggle to survive with everyone else. "Yes, I am a Brahmin, too," Rajesh would say,

and then add, mysteriously, "But I have done things no
Brahmin would have ever done."

I remember my first visit to his room, which was in
one of the derelict-looking hostels with piles of broken
furniture scattered on the front quad. The stairs to his
room were splattered with blood-red patterns made by
students spitting betel juice. In the assorted shabbiness
of his room—light from a naked bulb weakly falling on
scabby blue walls, unmade bed, discarded slippers,
rickety table, cheap denim jeans hanging limply from a
solitary nail in the wall, a bamboo bookstand tottering
under the weight of old newspapers—I noticed a jute
shoulder bag lying open on the ground, bulging with
crude pistols. No attempt had been made to conceal the
pistols, which seemed to belong as naturally to the
room as the green plastic bucket next to it. It made me
nervous; so did the hint of instability given by his
speech and manner, the long monologues, the uncon-
nected references to Wordsworth, to India. I began to
wish I saw less of him.

But it was hard to break off contact, even harder to
be indifferent to the innocent friendliness he exuded
every time I saw him. He often appeared at the library,
"checking up," he said, on whether I was being my studious self, or whether I went to the library to "ogle the
girls." I would try to avoid him by disappearing from
the library at the time he was likely to be there, but he
would then show up at a later hour. He also showed a
surprising amount of interest in my reading; surprising,
because although he had done an undergraduate
course in English, I rarely saw him reading anything

more than the Hindi newspapers scattered around the tea shops on the campus. "Edmund Wilson! Again! Why," he would ask with genuine bemusement, "are you always reading the same man?" He listened patiently while I tried to say a few explanatory words about the particular book or essay he had pointed to. He once caught me reading *To the Finland Station*, and I had to provide a crude summary, in fewer words than used by Wilson, of Trotsky's main ideas. I couldn't, of course, refuse; the thought of Rajesh's instability, the pistols in his room, always forced me to summon up a reasonably friendly response. It could be exhausting being with him at times. Why, I would wonder, did he, who seemed to have read little beyond Faiz and the Romantics, want to know so much about people so distant from us, like Trotsky or Bakunin? (More simply, why couldn't he spend his time with other people in the university?)

Rajesh was well-known in student circles. There was a special respect for him among other upper-caste students from nearby villages; lonely and vulnerable in what to them was the larger, intimidating world away from home, they saw in Rajesh a sympathetic fellow provincial and older protector. Rajesh fit the role rather well: he was physically bigger and stronger than most students on the campus; he had a certain reputation—a lot of people seemed to know about the pistols in his room; and it pleased him to be thought of as a godfatherlike figure.

A small crowd instantly gathered around him whenever I went out with him to a tea stall, and eagerly hung on to every word he spoke. He often talked about politics, the latest developments in Delhi, the current gossip about the size of a minister's wealth; he would repeat colorful stories about local politicians, the imaginative ways in which they had conned the World Bank or some other development agency, the bridges that were built only on paper, the roads that existed only in files.

Indeed, I often wondered—although he seemed content simply talking about politics—if he was not planning to be a politician himself: students with a popular mass base in the university who proved themselves capable of organizing strikes and demonstrations were often handpicked by local political bosses to contest elections to the local municipal corporation. He seemed to know people off campus as well; I once noticed in his room a couple of conspicuously affluent visitors who had driven to see him in a sinister-looking pale green Ambassador with tinted windows.

But I was preoccupied, particularly with Wilson's writings and their maze of cross-references which sent me scurrying from book to book in an effort to plug up at least some of what I felt were egregious gaps in my knowledge. One of the books I came across in this way was Flaubert's *Sentimental Education*, which I had read rather indifferently in a Penguin Classics edition some time back. Wilson's essay on the politics of Flaubert, collected in *The Triple Thinkers*, made me want to reread it. Now I found this account of an ambitious provincial's tryst with metropolitan glamour and disillusion full of the kind of subtle satisfactions that a neurotic adolescent sensibility would be especially susceptible to. I identified with Frédéric Moreau, the protagonist, with his large, passionate, but imprecise, longings, his indecisiveness, his aimlessness, his self-contempt. I cannot ever forget the sick feeling that came over me after I finished the novel late one evening at the library. I was only twenty, and much experience, and many more books, lay ahead of me. Yet I couldn't fail to recognize the intimations the novel gave me of the many stages of drift and futility I was encountering and was yet to encounter in my own life.

I recommended *Sentimental Education* to Rajesh one evening, and gave him a Xeroxed copy of Wilson's essay. I didn't expect him to read all of it; but he had been curious about Wilson, and I thought the essay was a good example of his writing. I didn't hear from him for a few weeks. My life went on as before. I left for the library early in the morning, and came back to a house reverberating with the exuberant jangling of sitars, the doleful twang of sarods, the hollow beat of tablas. I ate every evening with Panditji's wife, sitting cross-legged on the floor in her dark kitchen, awkwardly inhaling thick smoke from the wood fire, over which Shyam dextrously juggled hot chapatis from one calloused palm to another.

Later, back in my room, trying to read in the low-voltage light, I would hear the bells for evening prayers ring out from the adjacent temple. I spoke little to the Americans who, after their lessons with Panditji, came up to the roof to smoke opium. I already knew I could not share my intellectual discoveries with them. They hadn't heard of Edmund Wilson: one of them, a Princeton undergraduate, straining to recognize the name, thought I meant the biologist E. O. Wilson. The cultural figures they spoke about, and appeared to miss in the often oppressive alienness of this most ancient of Indian towns, were then unknown to me; it was to take me a few more years to find out who David Letterman was. But the Americans were, like me, whatever their reasons, refugees from the modern world of work and achievement, explorers of a world that antedated their own, and I was sympathetic to them.

Several weeks after I'd last seen him, Rajesh abruptly reappeared one afternoon at the library. He had been away, he said, on urgent work. Now he was on his way to visit his mother who lived in a village forty miles west of Benares. Would I come with him? I thought of making some excuse, but then I realized I needed some diversion and I said yes. Besides, I was curious about Rajesh's background, of which he had told me nothing until then. I could guess that he wasn't well-off, but one could have said the same for most students at the university.

We left one cold foggy morning on the small-gauge, steam-engined train that in those days used to run between Benares and Allahabad. A chilly wind, gritty with coal dust, blew in through the iron-barred windows as the train puffed and wheezed through an endless flat plain, stubbly fields stretching to tree-blurred horizons, coils of smoke torpid above ragged settlements of mud huts and half-built brick houses. The train was empty, and we stretched ourselves on hard wooden benches, wrapped from head to toe in coarse military blankets, and hurriedly sipped cardamom-scented tea that seemed to turn cold the moment the vendor lifted the kettle off his tiny coal stove. We got off at a small station populated entirely, it seemed, by mangy dogs. Another half-hour tonga ride from there, the horse's hooves clattering loudly against the tarmac road. Mango groves on both sides. Here and there, a few buildings: box-shaped houses of naked brick and mud huts with large courtyards where men slumbered on string cots; cold-storage warehouses; tiny shuttered shops. At an enclave of mud huts, swarthy blouseless women swept the common yard with brooms made of leafy neem twigs that left the earth raked over with crow's-feet patterns. Finally, at the end of a row of identical roadside buildings, there was Rajesh's own house, brick-walled, one room, poor—but what had I expected?

The door was opened by Rajesh's mother, a tiny shrunken woman in a widow's white saree. She looked frankly puzzled to see me at first, but suddenly grew very welcoming when Rajesh introduced me as a friend from the university. After the early morning light, it was dark and damp inside the high-ceilinged room. There was a solitary window, but it was closed. In one corner, partitioned off by a flimsy handloom saree, was the kitchen, where a few brass utensils dully gleamed in the dark, and where Rajesh's mother busied herself with breakfast. In another corner, under a sagging string cot, was a tin trunk, leprous with rust. There were religious calendars in garish colors on the walls:

Shiva, Krishna, Hanuman. I recall being unsettled by
that bare, lightless room, and its extreme poverty,
something not immediately apparent in Rajesh's life in
Benares.

Rajesh, who since the morning had become increasingly silent, left the room, and I sat in a straight-backed
wicker chair and talked to his mother. Both of us had to
speak very loudly to make ourselves heard above the
hissing sounds from the kerosene stove. It wasn't easy
to express sympathy in that high-pitched voice; and
sympathy was what was increasingly required of me as
she began to tell me stories from her past. She had been
widowed fifteen years ago when Rajesh was still a
child, and soon afterward her wealthy, feudal in-laws
had started to harass her. The house in which she lived
with her husband and son was taken away from her,
and they refused to give back the little dowry she had
brought with her. Her parents were dead, her brothers
too poor to support her. There was only Rajesh, who
had worked since he was thirteen, first in the maize
fields, and then at a carpet factory in Benares, where he
had gone to evening school and done well enough to
enter the university. The years had somehow passed.

But now she was worried. Rajesh, she felt, had
reached a dead end. There were no more openings for
him. All the jobs these days were going to low-caste
people. And not only did Rajesh have the wrong kind
of caste, he had no connections anywhere for a government job. And, she added with a touch of old Brahmin
pride, he had too much self-respect to work for low-
caste shopkeepers and businessmen.

How little of his past I had known! I knew a bit about those carpet factories; they had been in the papers after some human rights organizations petitioned the courts to prohibit them from using child labor. There had been pictures of large-eyed, frightened-looking children in dungeon-like rooms, framed against their exquisite handiworks. I was shocked to know that Rajesh had been one of them. The tormenting private memories of childhood that he carried within himself seemed unimaginable.

On the train back to Benares, Rajesh broke his silence to say that he had read *Sentimental Education*, and that it was a story he knew well. "*Yeh meri duniya ki kahani hai. Main in logo ko janta hoon,*" he said, in Hindi. "It is the story of my world. I know these people well." He gave me a hard look. "Your hero, Edmund Wilson," he added, in English, "he also knows them."

What did Rajesh, a student in a provincial Indian university in the late 1980s, have in common with Frédéric Moreau or any of the doomed members of his generation in this novel of mid-nineteenth-century Paris? As it happened, I didn't ask him to explain. I had already been made to feel awkward by the unexpected disclosures about his past. And then the day had been somewhat exhausting. We talked, desultorily, of other things, and parted in Benares.

I was in Benares again two years later, when I heard about Rajesh.

The man who told me, someone I remembered as one of Rajesh's hangers-on, appeared surprised that I didn't already know that he had been a member of a criminal gang specializing in debt collection on behalf of a group of local moneylenders and businessmen. That explains his mysterious absences from Benares, I thought, as well as the pistols in his room and the sinister-looking Ambassador with tinted windows.

It was, the man said, a good, steady business: once confronted with the possibility of violence, people paid up very quickly, without involving the police. But then Rajesh had graduated to something riskier—and here, although shocked and bewildered by what I had been told, and fully expecting the worst now, I could not take it in.

At some stage, the man said, dramatically pausing after every word, Rajesh had turned himself into a contract killer. It was an extremely well-paid profession; also, a well-connected one. You worked for small-time contractors who in turn worked for wealthy industrialists and also did favors for local political bosses who did not always rely on their own "private armies" (the local term for loyal henchmen) for certain jobs. You got to know everyone well after a few years in the business. You worked for all these important people, yet you were always on your own. The chances of survival weren't very high. Sooner or later, the police came to hear of you. Fierce loyalties of caste and clan ensured that every murder would be avenged. It was what would one day happen to Rajesh, he said. In a typical ambush of the kind often reported in the local papers, he would be on his motorcycle when four men would surround him at a busy intersection in the old city, and shoot him dead. The prurient excitement on the man's face filled me with disgust and anger.

I never did hear what happened to Rajesh. Such stories were in the newspapers every day. But it took me a while to sort out my confused feelings. I kept seeing Rajesh at that busy crossing, trapped in the dense swarm of scooters, cycle rickshaws, bullock carts, cars, buses, trucks, and bicycles, the four men converging upon him, producing crude pistols from their pockets . . .

Rajesh had bewildered me: his self-consciousness about his Brahmin identity, the pistols in his room, his constant talk of the void. I could now see that he had been struggling to make sense of his life, to connect the disparate elements that existed in it; but so, in a different way, was I.

Then a few months ago I thought of writing something on Edmund Wilson. I had tried before, in 1995, the year of Wilson's centenary, but what I wrote seemed to me too much like a reprise of what a lot of other people had already said about him. But then I was trying to write about him in the way an American or European writer would have. What I had in mind was a straightforward exposition of Wilson's key books. It didn't occur to me that a separate narrative probably existed in my private discovery of Wilson's writings in a dusty old library in the ancient town of Benares.

Now I was again looking for material on Wilson in preparation for another attempt when, browsing through old papers, I came across a Xeroxed copy of his essay on Flaubert's politics. It looked familiar. Idly flipping through the essay, I came to the pages on *Sentimental Education*, where I saw some passages underlined in red. As I am not in the habit of marking up a printed text, I wondered who had done this. I read the underlined sentences:

> Frédéric is only the more refined as well as the more incompetent side of the middle-class mediocrity of which the dubious promoter represents the more flashy and active aspect. And so in the case of the other characters, the journalists and the artists, the members of the various political factions, the remnants of the old nobility, Frédéric finds the same shoddiness and lack of principle which are gradually revealed in himself. . . .

On another page the underlined passage read:

> Flaubert's novel plants deep in our mind an idea which we never quite get rid of: the suspicion that our middle-class society of manufacturers, businessmen, and bankers, of people who live on or deal in investments, so far from being redeemed by its culture, has ended by cheapening and invalidating all the departments of culture, political, scientific, artistic, and religious, as well as corrupting and weakening the ordinary human relations: love, friendship, and loyalty to cause—till the whole civilization seems to dwindle.

The passage offered a small glimpse of Wilson's way of finding the sources and effects of literature in the overlap between individual states of mind and specific historical realities. But I hadn't noticed it when I first came across it. I read it again and thought about the red underlinings. And then, after almost seven years, Rajesh strode back into my consciousness. I remembered the afternoon I had given *Sentimental Education* and Wilson's essay to him; I remembered his words to me on the train, words I dismissed as exaggeration, the hard, determined look on his face as he said, "It is the story of my world. I know these people well. Your hero, Edmund Wilson, he also knows them."

What had he meant by that?

The question did not leave me. And there came a time when I began to think I had understood very little, and misunderstood much, during those months in Benares. I thought of the day I went to visit Rajesh's village and I at last saw that there had been a purpose behind Rajesh's invitation to his home, his decision to so frankly reveal his life to me. Even the cryptic remarks about *Sentimental Education* and Wilson on the train: he wanted me to know that not only had he read the novel, he had drawn, with Wilson's help, his own conclusions from it.

In the hard and mean world he had lived in, first as a child laborer and then as hired criminal for politicians and businessmen, Rajesh would have come to know well the grimy underside of middle-class society. What became clearer to me now was how quick he had been to recognize that the society Flaubert and Wilson wrote about wasn't much different from the one he inhabited in Benares: "It's the story of my world," he had said. I couldn't see it then but in Benares I had been among people who, like Frédéric Moreau and his friends, had either disowned or, in many cases, moved away from their provincial origins in order to realize their dreams of success in the bourgeois world. Only a handful of them were able to get anywhere near to realizing their dreams while the rest saw their ambitions dwindle away over the years in successive disappointments. The degradation of bribery, sycophancy, and nepotism that people were forced into in their hunt for jobs was undermining in itself: so pervasive was the corruption around them that neither those who succeeded nor those who failed were able to escape its taint.

The small, unnoticed tragedies of thwarted hopes and ideals Flaubert wrote about in *Sentimental Education* were all around us. And this awareness— which was also mine but which I tried to evade through, ironically, the kind of obsessive reading that had led me to the novel in the first place—had been Rajesh's private key to the book. Thus, where I saw only the reflection of a personal neurosis—the character of Frédéric in particular embodying my sense of inadequacy, my severe self-image—he had discovered a social and psychological environment that was similar to the one he lived in.

That discovery did honor to both Flaubert and Wilson. The world we knew in Benares was many years away from those of the French novelist and the American critic. Yet—and this was a measure of their greatness—they seemed to have had an accurate, if bitter, knowledge of its peculiar human ordeals and futility. It was a knowledge Rajesh himself arrived at by a somewhat different route. "To fully appreciate the book," Wilson had written of *Sentimental Education*, "one must have had time to see something of life." It sounds like a general sort of adage; but Rajesh exemplified its truth even as he moved into another world, taking what in retrospect look like all the wrong turns. Rajesh had known how to connect whatever little he read to the world around himself, much in the same way Wilson had done in his essay, and in his other writings, which reveal a symbiotic relationship between life and literature that I, despite all my reading, was not fully to grasp until long after I had left Benares and thought again of that time of hopeful, confused striving when I first read Edmund Wilson.

Pankaj
Mishra

- - - - -

A New,
Nuclear,
India?

1

- - - - -

IN EARLY MARCH this year, India had a new
government. It was the seventh to be formed in less
than a decade; and it seemed for the first few weeks as
though the eighth was not very far off. The Hindu
nationalist BJP (Indian People's Party) and its allies, in
office for a total of thirteen days in 1996, had a hard
time mustering the required majority in the parliament
and then came under heavy pressure from its coalition
partners.

The leader of one of the BJP's more important allies,
from the South Indian state of Tamil Nadu, an eccentric former film star called Jayalalitha, whose party has
eighteen seats in the parliament, bargained hard to
have her supporters included in the central cabinet, and
started attacking the new prime minister, Atal Bihari
Vajpayee, for forcing out one of them after he was
charged in a corruption case. The Prime Minister was
slow to fire two others of his coalition partners—both
facing corruption charges. Other partners branded him
as weak and indecisive, and then made their own
demands; one called for the dismissal of an elected state

government. Rumors about the impending collapse of the government in the forthcoming parliamentary session had started going around when in mid-May the government resorted to an old bogey—national security—to buy time for itself.

After four wars with China and Pakistan in the last fifty years, and several violent separatist movements, a general consensus exists in India on issues of national security: no political party can question the country's huge defense expenditure (nine soldiers for every doctor) without being called antinational. Thus saber rattling and rhetoric about threats to India's security from China and Pakistan have become favorite ruses of beleaguered Indian governments. India's first nuclear test in 1974 came in handy for Indira Gandhi when she was facing a crippling railway strike (the first of the political challenges that eventually led her to suspend civil rights in 1975). When faced with growing allegations of incompetence and corruption in 1987, Rajiv Gandhi had military exercises held provocatively close to the Pakistan border and made political capital out of the resulting tension. The jingoism of a weak coalition government almost forced India into war with Pakistan in 1989.

Some sort of Indian response was in the cards once Pakistan, which acquired nuclear capability in the 1980s, announced in April the successful test-firing of an IRBM (Intermediate Range Ballistic Missile) capable of carrying nuclear warheads as deep as 1,000 miles into Indian territory. On May 28 Pakistan announced that it had carried out nuclear tests. But few people expected the response to the April announcement to be as emphatic—and, for the BJP, well-timed—as India's five nuclear tests in early May, which radically redefined India's relationship with the world.

A low-intensity military conflict with Pakistan has been going on for the last decade in the remote northern reaches of the Himalayas; and there is increasing evidence that China has shared some of its nuclear knowledge with Pakistan. However, the government's claim, in a letter from Vajpayee to Bill Clinton, that India's nuclear testing was meant to dramatize the country's security concerns before an international audience is only part of the truth.

India acquired nuclear capability in 1974 with what it termed a peaceful explosion: "The Buddha has smiled" was the coded message of success to the then prime minister, Indira Gandhi; more incongruous words have been used since then to defend and justify India's nuclear policies. Successive Indian governments have refused to sign the NPT (Nuclear Non-Proliferation Treaty) and CTBT (Comprehensive Test Ban Treaty) on the grounds that these treaties discriminated against the countries outside the group of five nuclear powers (US, Russia, France, China, and Britain): an exclusive club formed of countries that had exploded a nuclear device before January 1, 1967. The Indians have long wanted to gain entry into that club: the assumption is that official recognition of their status as a nuclear power (while facilitating India's much-sought-after permanent seat in the Security Council) would free them from the discriminatory strictures imposed on signatories of the treaties, and would bring them the special privileges and rights of other club members, which include the right to privately refine and develop nuclear armories without testing.

Much rhetoric about the need for a disarmament schedule and attacks on Western countries for their hypocrisy have been heard from the Indian representatives at various international forums on the nuclear question in recent years, while India, according to intelligence agencies in the US and Europe, was busily accumulating enough plutonium to make several bombs. Much is also known about India's ambitious plans to build nuclear submarines and missiles, including an ICBM. Clandestine work on developing nuclear weapons has gone on for a long time. But India so far had been careful to keep up an image of self-restraint by not formally declaring or displaying its military capacity, especially recently, when relations with Pakistan and China have generally been better than at any other time in the last two decades.

The response in India makes it clear that it was more a local than an international audience that the BJP had in mind. The nuclear tests have been extremely popular, particularly among the urban middle class, the BJP's prime constituency: initial opinion polls showed an approval rating of 91 percent; the figure may have gone down slightly since then. In the period following 1984—when the party was gaining strength—the bloody terrorist movements in Punjab and Kashmir (which caused an estimated 40,000 deaths) and the assassinations of Indira and Rajiv Gandhi as well as other Indian leaders exacerbated an underlying paranoia toward Pakistan among middle-class Hindus. In his letter to Clinton, Vajpayee described Pakistan as "bitter"—without giving a reason for that bitterness. But many Indians think it has to do with Pakistan's humiliating defeat in the war over Bangladesh in 1971. They also believe that a vengeful Pakistan has fomented and aided all the violent secessionist movements in India in the last two decades—has, in effect, conducted a proxy war against India.

To large sections of the educated middle class, the nuclear tests—one of which, so the Indians claim, signaled hydrogen bomb capability—represent a toughness toward Pakistan that they have long wanted. Not unexpectedly, the hard-line home minister, L. K. Advani, has talked of punishing Pakistan for its support of Muslim secessionists in Kashmir. The tests removed a feeling of "national weakness" among Indians, a BJP spokesman said. This is why criticism of the Prime Minister virtually ceased for a while after the tests: he was now praised, even by his recent opponents, for being courageous and decisive, for having done what no previous government could do, and for having also in the process delivered on the BJP's electoral promise to exercise what is referred to in India as the nuclear option.

Most Indian newspapers, although not all, have welcomed the tests and joined the government in deploring the double standard of the five nuclear powers that would deny India what they themselves possess in abundance. The opposition parties at first felt themselves compelled to go along with the public mood; the Congress Party, under Sonia Gandhi, first considered opposing the tests, then supported them, and, after the huge surge in the BJP's popularity, which threatens them directly, is now slowly modifying its position. Some parties that formed the previous government even tried to claim credit for the tests by saying that they had prepared the ground for them. Among political parties, only the Communists at first dared to raise questions about the BJP's motives and timing. The nationwide euphoria over what is seen as a big step for India in the world is now likely to keep the BJP's fickle partners in line: they will be nervous about the possibility of another round of elections, which may return the BJP to power with a clear majority, for dramatic international sanctions would stoke a defensive patriotism within India that the BJP is well placed to exploit.

After the first wave of euphoria and celebrations, dissenting voices, however, are beginning to be heard. Scientists from two prestigious Indian institutions, the Tata Institute of Fundamental Research and the Institute of Mathematical Research, have published protests against the tests, pointing to the incongruity of a third-world nation aspiring to first-world nuclear status. India's two most respected news magazines, *Outlook* and *Frontline*, have expressed deep skepticism about the tests; these magazines represent the opposition to the tests among India's small metropolitan intelligentsia.

But whipping up xenophobia and patriotic fervor among the middle class alone cannot ensure the government's stability. Troublesome partners are quiet only for now. What is clear is that nuclear muscle-flexing will not go any way toward solving India's gigantic problems of poverty, illiteracy, malnutrition, and overpopulation. These problems are best addressed by stable governments. Whether the present government, despite its current popularity, can last its full five-year term is doubtful.

2

- - - - -

THE CONGRESS PARTY that led the movement for freedom from the British did provide India that essential stability for forty-three out of its fifty years, when it was the only pan-Indian political force in sight. But its decline in recent years has led to a fast turnover of political parties and personalities, with coalitions springing up overnight and members of parliament changing parties twice or thrice in a single day amid rumors of payoffs and fierce competition. Late last year, the BJP did look as if it might replace the Congress, which was seriously weakened by dissidence, while its leaders were preoccupied with fighting corruption charges in the courts. After a long run in power it won just enough seats in the elections two years ago to enable it to support, from outside, a rag-tag coalition of regional and left-wing parties and keep its main competition, the BJP, at bay. For the 1998 elections, the BJP was set to achieve an easy majority in the parliament.

Then, shortly after Christmas, Sonia Gandhi announced her decision to campaign for the Congress, the party of her late husband and mother-in-law, and the situation changed for both the Congress and the BJP. In Goa, where I heard Sonia Gandhi speak at an election rally, I met an Italian journalist. He was part of the large contingent of Italian reporters and photographers trailing Mrs. Gandhi on her campaign tour across India. He already had his story. Sonia Gandhi was big news in Italy, but it wasn't her politics anyone was interested in. It was the glamour of the dynasty, the glamour of royalty in democracy, the journalist said. It's like—what's the English word?—yes, soap opera. Even Oriana Fallacci, he said, couldn't have thought up a plot where a middle-class woman from a small town near Turin tries to rescue India's oldest political party from extinction.

The rescue seemed improbable at the time. For one, Sonia Gandhi herself was under a cloud. Fresh revelations about the Bofors scandal that unseated her husband in 1989 implicated one of Mrs. Gandhi's closest Italian friends in Delhi as having served as a middleman in the illegal commissions allegedly paid to Rajiv Gandhi in a deal with the Swedish artillery manufacturers.

Mrs. Gandhi's decision to campaign for the Congress came after a prolonged period during which she was repeatedly importuned to take an active role in politics by fractious party leaders who would only agree with one another about the need to make Mrs. Gandhi supreme leader. The pictures of white-clad Congress leaders contorting themselves into postures of obeisance on Mrs. Gandhi's impeccably mowed front lawn became a regular feature in the morning papers. Their exertions were prompted by the fact that the Congress Party had declined more rapidly in the last seven years, when no member of the Nehru-Gandhi family was at its helm, than at any other time in its 113-year history.

Even before she was officially appointed the president of the party, its relentless wooing of Mrs. Gandhi bestowed a lot of authority on her. Her reticence only added to her mysterious aura; she now commands a curiously Olympian extraconstitutional status in New Delhi. Her special privileges were maintained even during the two years the Congress was out of power. Visiting heads of state continued to call upon her at her house in Delhi's most exclusive district; she was seated along with former prime ministers at official occasions; government regulations were circumvented in order to keep the Rajiv Gandhi Foundation well supplied with money.

During the campaign, many commentators discounted Mrs. Gandhi's influence over the electorate on the grounds that the political climate had greatly changed since the heyday of the Nehru–Gandhi dynasty, when Pandit Nehru or Indira Gandhi, by sheer personal charisma, could carry with them such utterly diverse groups as the Brahmins and the Dalits (low-caste Hindus)—not to mention the Muslims who used to vote en masse for the Congress. The feeling was that the old days of consensus politics were now gone, and that the Indian electorate had entered a new phase of maturity. To the stereotypical pictures of the long queues of expectant villagers outside polling booths— perhaps the most powerful and misleading image of Indian democracy yet—were added pictures of the low-caste shoemaker in a small village, someone who was no longer tempted by the Congress's promises or dazzled by the Nehru–Gandhi name. He recognized his self-interest and knew how he could protect it by voting for men of his own caste. The representatives he voted for, genuine sons of the soil, were said to constitute a new, aggressive class of political leaders.

But the election demonstrated how much such analyses underestimated the great appeal of the Nehru–Gandhi dynasty. Mrs. Gandhi evoked a rapturous response almost everywhere she went—and she went to a lot of places, four or five every day. Huge crowds— up to 100,000 strong—waited for long hours in all extremes of weather for her helicopter to arrive. A single gesture from her two children sent the crowds into frenzies of applause and cheering. People wept on TV while listening to her speak about the sacrifices of her assassinated relatives; tearful mothers pointed to the resemblance, which is actually very slight, between Mrs. Gandhi's son, Rahul, and his father.

Sonia Gandhi's Italian background, at first thought to be a liability, and her association with the Nehru–Gandhi dynasty only made things easier for her. No Indian leader outside that dynasty has been able to effectively project for himself the pan-Indian identity it almost effortlessly possesses; or to avoid the taint of regionalism, casteism, or communalism. Nehru was a Brahmin from Kashmir but resident in Allahabad, an Urdu-speaker, and an Anglophile. Indira Gandhi was educated partly in Switzerland and England, and married a Parsi man. Her half-Parsi son, Rajiv Gandhi, went to Cambridge and married an Italian woman. The mélange of cultural identities is unusual in Indian politics; also, glamorous. So it is that mass perceptions of the Nehru–Gandhi family usually coincide with the family's careful self-presentation: secular, cosmopolitan, and possessed of a larger (for Nehru, almost mystical) feeling for India and Indians, above all for the toiling millions.

Public memory in India is notoriously short (Indira Gandhi was back in power three years after the worst excesses of the Emergency), and few people remember much of the dynasty's political record. Nehru, who died in 1964, is now a legendary figure to most Indians. Sanjay Gandhi's ruthless uprooting of whole communities in Delhi; Mrs. Gandhi's cynical *Realpolitik* in Punjab, where she encouraged Sikh militancy to unsettle an opposition government; Rajiv Gandhi's disastrous military adventures in Sri Lanka: all these events, mulled over by political analysts, seem not to matter much to the masses. What has proved most persistent in memory is the brutal manner of the deaths of Mrs. Gandhi and her sons, the patched-up corpses, the images from their funerals (all but the earliest telecast live across India), of first a grief-stricken mother, then a son, and then his widow and tender-aged children.

Sonia Gandhi used this memory to good effect, and her speeches, which blended melodramatic legend-making with harsh facts about poverty and under-development, went down well in a predominantly rural country—particularly among women—oppressed by high inflation, lawlessness, and corruption. It was a campaigning style that owed much to her mother-in-law, who when pushed into a tight corner would send an emotional message of hope and consolation that bypassed preexisting political and economic realities and reached out directly to the masses. Like Indira, who was hailed as Durga (the Hindu goddess who is the incarnation of female energy) after the defeat of Pakistan in the 1971 war, Sonia Gandhi was well aware of the symbolic value of presenting herself as a benevolent mother-goddess figure—a tactic that, to judge by the number of prominent women leaders in Sri Lanka, Myanmar, Pakistan, and Bangladesh, appears to work well not only in India but throughout South Asia.

Because of Mrs. Gandhi's last-minute efforts, Congress was granted a reprieve. It recovered, thanks to her, some of its old support among the poorest of voters and among Muslims. Instead of being reduced to double digits in the parliament, it has managed to remain a major player by winning 142 seats, while the BJP won 179 seats. In the months ahead, the Congress at least theoretically has enough power to topple governments, or even, with a bit of horse-trading, to form its own government, with Sonia Gandhi again in her now customary role of aloof and mysterious arbiter.

Nevertheless, particularly in view of the strong support for the BJP after the nuclear tests, Congress still looks like a party in its last stages: a party with one attractive figure, but with no program, or even leaders—some of its old stalwarts were defeated in the recent elections and the younger ones have been unable to rise above the party culture of sycophancy and internecine squabbling.

For much of the time it ruled India, the Congress had no effective opposition in the parliament.[1] But this advantage has not been good for Indian democracy, and it has been even less good for the Congress. Mahatma Gandhi may have had in mind the unhealthy consequences of the Congress's hegemony when he said he wanted it to disband after Independence.

The Insider by P.V. Narasimha Rao, the last Congress prime minister of India—who served between 1991 and 1996—is a remarkable new book that tells us more about the inner workings of the Congress, and hence India's rulers, than any other book in the last fifty years.[2] Rao is a scholar and linguist of some repute in his native language, Telugu, and has spent five decades in national politics, during which time he worked very closely with the Nehru–Gandhi family. Few Indian politicians, active or retired, ever write books, and those who do are careful to spill only a few largely irrelevant beans.

---

1. The only example offered by democratic countries of this is the long, corrupt, and corrupting monopoly on power of Mexico's PRI.

2. New Delhi: Viking/Penguin India, 1998.

The Insider is the first attempt of its sort: an account of Indian politics that is both personal and broadly historical, and also, startlingly, has the ring of truth. It raises serious doubts about the nature of Indian democracy, the way India has been ruled by the Congress, the increasing decay and corruption. In the process, it exposes the wide gap that exists between the appearance and reality of India's Westminster-inspired democratic institutions. According to Rao, with India's independence, "imperial authority... merely turned into Central authority.... Neither the democratic nor the federal principle had taken root to supplant the feudal ethos ... [of] past centuries; the concept of kingship... was ingrained in the collective consciousness.... Democracy in action at best consisted of the question: Who should reign?"

Thus "chieftains appeared in the garb of chief ministers." A good part of *The Insider* is taken up with dramatizing the attributes of one such chieftain called Mahendranath: "iron-handed administration, cruelty, sadism, egocentrism, intolerance, arbitrariness, aggressiveness, ruthlessness, sexual license as of right ... and an utter contempt for the people except, of course, at election time." "Umpteen Mahendranaths," Rao asserts, "[dotted] the length and breadth of the country." One of them is Chaudhury, a politician "with no particular ideology other than power." Chaudhury does not "believe in any of the rhetoric of the Party's statements and resolutions. In a country of sub-naked illiterates living in sub-human conditions, what is the relevance of any ideology, he often asked.... We wanted to rule our own country, so we made the British quit. That doesn't mean we have to reject British techniques of administration. Rule with a firm hand and to hell with ideology!"

The main character of *The Insider* is Anand, who is very clearly based on Rao. From his childhood in a South Indian village, and then as a student inspired by the idealism of Gandhi and Nehru, Anand charts Rao's own journey through the Congress to the highest executive job in the country. Shrewdly, Rao has written a book that is halfway between autobiography and fiction. Although recently sidelined within the Congress, Rao is still an active member of the party under Sonia Gandhi; he also has several corruption cases against him in the courts. Straightforward autobiography would have inhibited him; fiction probably has enabled him to be less economical with the truth.

It has also allowed him to reinvent himself. Anand is portrayed as being disenchanted by the cynical power games played by his party, by the skulduggery, hypocrisy, and corruption that are the Congress's legacy to the Indian state. This is disingenuous. Rao himself was a player, and a rather good one at that: one of the charges he is currently facing is that, as prime minister of India from 1991 to 1996, he bought five MPs for $1.2 million each from a regional party in order to prop up his minority government.

It is Rao's larger view of his subject that redeems his frequently ponderous narrative and pedestrian prose. Anand, as minister for land reforms in a provincial government, is eloquent on the government's failure in the 1950s to redistribute cultivable land: once again, high-minded programs originating from Nehru's office in Delhi became victims of vested interests within the Congress. The landlord class, from which many of the Congress's leaders came, could not be antagonized; and thus the cruel economic disparities of rural India continued even as the men of the Congress learned to mouth the rhetoric of socialism.

Various books have been written about Nehru's seventeen years in power, but they tend to focus on events in New Delhi, on what Nehru thought or said or believed. Anand, as a provincial politician, describes from a previously unavailable perspective those years when various corrupt party bosses turned not only the Congress but also Indian democracy itself into a bargaining counter for special-interest groups, each narrowly organized around specific castes, religions, and regions. (Set in the early 1950s, Vikram Seth's *A Suitable Boy*[3] also offers a convincing fictional account of these competitive political tendencies within North India.)

What becomes clear through Rao's narrative is that Nehru's paternalistic style of governance strengthened an old Indian trait of looking up to remote, regal figures for ways out of social and economic distress; it set the stage for the populist personality politics of his daughter, Indira Gandhi, who, no democrat herself, took on the party bosses, and did so by the simple

---

3. HarperCollins, 1993.

expedient of appealing to the masses over their heads. *Garibi Hatao* ("Abolish Poverty"): this was the seemingly obvious (for India) and effective slogan with which she won in 1971 one of the largest majorities ever secured in the Indian parliament.

Rao touches briefly on Mrs. Gandhi's autocratic tendencies, her grooming of businessmen-politicians much like his character, Gopi Kishen, who, while not quite in Mrs. Gandhi's so-called kitchen cabinet, her coterie of sycophants, "procured provisions for the kitchen." During the days of the British Raj, Rao writes with heavy irony, Gopi Kishen was "initiated into the mysteries of politics-cum-business" by his millionaire father, who made him spend a few days in jail with other freedom fighters so that when he came out his record of patriotism would help him rise fast and high up the political and business ladder. The irony here may seem at first overdone, but Rao is merely being truthful about a very common kind of self-serving politician that came to rule India after Independence.

Rao concludes his narrative in 1973, two years before Mrs. Gandhi's infamous Emergency was declared—an act Rao now says he disapproved of, if not enough for him to think of leaving the party. The abrupt conclusion comes as a disappointment because the real story, as we know it, accelerated only after 1973. Rao has promised a sequel, but whether he'll tell the full truth about Mrs. Gandhi's autocratic rule will probably depend on whether he is allowed greater power within the Congress by Sonia Gandhi.

Mrs. Gandhi's response to a court conviction for

electoral malfeasance was to arrest opposition leaders clamoring for her resignation, suspend civil rights, and encourage a cult of the supreme leader around herself: "Indira is India" was the popular slogan of the time. Her ambitious son Sanjay bullied his way around democratic procedures and become a proxy prime minister. In the early 1980s, Mrs. Gandhi began to covertly support Sikh militancy in Punjab and Tamil militancy in Sri Lanka in order to gain the votes of local Hindus. Both strategies were to backfire. She was assassinated by her own Sikh bodyguards in 1984, a few months after ordering the disastrous invasion of the Golden Temple in Amritsar. The conspiracy to kill her son, Rajiv Gandhi, in 1991, was the work of Tamil secessionists who had been originally outfitted and trained by the Indian army on Mrs. Gandhi's orders.

Rajiv Gandhi, an airline pilot by profession, won the largest-ever parliamentary majority in an election held a month after his mother died—an election Mrs. Gandhi was expected to lose—but soon squandered his immense goodwill through a series of blunders. Senior Congress leaders organized the mass executions in Delhi of 3,000 Sikhs following his mother's death, but Rajiv had only this to say: "When a giant tree falls, the earth shakes." The Sikhs have yet to forgive the Congress for the killings.

A lover of gadgets, Rajiv built up a personal coterie of smooth-talking young friends and advisors who knew more about the latest Apple notebook than about India's drinking-water problem. The public exchequer was drained by flamboyant and wasteful ventures designed to take India into the twenty-first century—a pet theme of Rajiv's. He committed the Indian army to a bloody and futile war in Sri Lanka, rigged elections in Kashmir. But it was the scandal over kickbacks from Bofors that inflicted the greatest damage. He lost the 1989 elections, and a coalition of opposition parties took over from the Congress.

3

- - - - -

OF THAT COALITION, whose constituent parties frequently change their names, and which was in office for another short-lived term, from May 1996 to December 1997, only the Communist parties have managed to retain their longstanding electoral base in West Bengal and Kerala. The rest of the parties have split and split again—sometimes until they are close to extinction. It is the BJP—part of the coalition in 1989 before it struck out on its own in 1990 with what is called the Ayodhya movement—that has most profited from the Congress Party's present difficulties.

In December 1992, the BJP achieved international notoriety when a mob, in a fit of frenzy, demolished the Babri Masjid (or mosque) in Ayodhya in the state of Uttar Pradesh. Built in the early sixteenth century, the mosque is commonly believed to be the work of the Central Asian conqueror and first Moghul emperor, Babur; and like many such Islamic monuments of conquest in North India, it was constructed out of materials from the Hindu temple that stood on the same site before being destroyed to make way for the mosque.

Hindu legend identified the site as the birthplace of Lord Rama, one of the most revered Hindu gods, and there had been some talk in the last few decades among some religious Hindus about moving the mosque to an adjacent site and rebuilding the temple on the spot. The BJP saw the political potential in the talk, saw how the issue could be used to bring into its fold many Hindu voters disenchanted with the Congress. It exploited the Ayodhya issue heavily, which may have contributed to the anti-Congress wave in 1989, when the number of BJP seats in the parliament rose from two to eighty-five.

Three years later, the mosque was demolished, burdening the BJP with the fundamentalist label, an especially damaging one in view of the concurrent rise of militant fundamentalism in Algeria, Egypt, and Iran. It has to be said, however, that when applied to an Indian situation, the label simplifies far too much; nor does it help to explain the BJP, which paradoxically claims to be in opposition to theocracy of any sort, has long termed caste, the mainstay of Hindu society, a social evil, and has presented itself as a guardian of true—as opposed to what it considers the Congress's "pseudo"—secularism.

To see the demolition as defining the BJP's essential character and intentions is to ignore, among other things, its surprisingly flexible, if not mercurial, rhetoric. In recent elections, it has presented itself as a party for radical change, committed to building a secular, progressive India where all citizens will be equal and there shall be no discrimination based on race, caste, or religion. Accordingly, the new Prime Minister in his first speech after the election declared war on hunger, fear, and corruption. Skeptics see these self-presentations as an attempt to duplicate the Congress's now-diminished ability to be all things to everyone, and they may be right. In the last several years, the BJP has followed the Congress in accommodating a great many contradictory aspirations and impulses in its bid for power.

But it seems fair to say that the demolition came as a surprise to many of the BJP's own leaders, if not to the party's extremist allies, such as Shiv Sena, the Hindu party from Bombay led by a former cartoonist and self-confessed admirer of Hitler called Bal Thackeray. Thackeray himself first acquired prominence in the 1970s with his crusade against South Indian, mostly Hindu, immigrants in Bombay, whom he accused of taking all the jobs away from the local Marathi-speaking population. Before the demolition, Thackeray switched to anti-Muslim rabble-rousing, quite independently of the BJP, and with a much cruder line: Muslims should support India in cricket matches with Pakistan, he said, or they should get out of the country and go to Pakistan.

Thackeray was quick to lend his support to the BJP on the Ayodhya issue; and the BJP, eager to create a base for itself in the state of Maharastra (of which Bombay is the capital city), allied itself successfully with

247

the Shiv Sena against the Congress in state elections in the early Nineties. Thackeray vigorously claimed sole credit for the demolition, for which he said his men in Ayodhya had been secretly trained, although the Shiv Sena was joined in destroying the mosque by members of various Hindu lumpen and millenarian groups who, unlike Shiv Sena, were part of the original movement to rebuild the temple and felt frustrated over the lack of progress in the BJP's attempts to reclaim the site.

For the BJP itself the demolition was a public relations disaster.[4] BJP governments in four Indian states were immediately dismissed by the president, acting on the advice of the prime minister, Narasimha Rao, who was himself under pressure from his cabinet to act decisively against the BJP. Senior leaders of the party were imprisoned and charged with criminal offenses. What had started out as a political movement designed to attract Hindu voters in large numbers had got badly out of hand. The BJP has yet to offer an explanation for the violence in Ayodhya, in which several members of the media were badly injured: statements from the party leaders still range between confused regret and aggressive self-righteousness.

The demolition of the mosque was a serious setback: in an election held in Uttar Pradesh soon after, the party did badly. Nor did the violent rioting between Hindus and Muslims that preceded and followed the demolition—the worst of it in Bombay, where the Shiv

---

4. In an interview soon after the demolition of the Babri Masjid, Vajpayee described the event as a "Himalayan blunder."

Sena ran amok, and retaliatory bombings organized by Muslim mafia dons in the Middle East and Pakistan killed 300 people in one day—do much for the party's image among the then-emerging middle classes, who wanted, more than anything else, a stable social environment in which to make money. This is doubtless why the party, while reminding voters of its promise to build a grand temple in Ayodhya, has so far done nothing about it. The temple issue featured in the BJP's electoral manifesto, but it has been pointedly excluded from the National Agenda drawn up since. "Where is Ayodhya?": this was Vajpayee's response to a TV interviewer wanting to know his plans.

Indeed, the party's original theme of exploiting popular awareness of past Hindu defeats and humiliations seems very much in cold storage at present. An awareness of history that reaches back four centuries is normally a rare thing in India. But the depredations of its Islamic conquerors have been a heavy presence in the imaginations of the Hindu educated middle class since the late nineteenth century, when Hindus educated at British-style colleges and universities first arrived at a new emotional idea of India through their contact with European ideas of nationalism. Many of the great Hindu reformers of the time, such as Swami Vivekanand and Swami Dayanand, both of them part of the BJP's pantheon, have recorded their troubled awareness of India's past and present degradation under Muslim and British rule, of what they saw as the disunity, backwardness, and progressive enfeeblement of the Hindus. Invariably, they saw India's salvation in a regenerated, politically organized, and assertive Hinduism.

The problem then as now is that Hinduism, with its plethora of diverse and contradictory traditions, its millions of gods and goddesses, its complicated caste hierarchy, is a highly amorphous religion—not so much a religion, in fact, as a way of life. As the Indian social critic Ashis Nandy puts it, one can only be a Hindu insofar as one is not a Hindu. The sheer diversity of Hindu practices makes it hard, if not impossible, to organize them around the lines of monotheistic, egalitarian religions like Islam and Christianity. The BJP, despite its best effort to semiticize Hinduism by harping on a single god (Lord Rama) and a single holy scripture (the Ramayana), can't deal with that problem. It has been struggling instead to find a large enough constituency for its central theme of *Hindutva*, cultural nationalism.

It is not easy to figure out what the BJP means by *Hindutva*; and matters are not helped by semantic confusions around the word "Hindu," which the BJP's ideologues insist is a cultural rather than religious category, including in the term converts from Hinduism, the 13 percent of India's population that is mainly Muslim, Sikh, and Christian—in effect all those who inhabit the *punya bhumi* (sacred land) of India. (The father of India's missile program, and one of the key figures behind the nuclear tests, is a Muslim scientist who could serve as an example of the kind of Muslims the BJP likes: deeply nationalist and steeped in India's great epics.)

When asked to explain *Hindutva*, the BJP's ideologues usually lapse into exaggerated talk of India's
golden age, when great discoveries in science and
astronomy were made, and every village was a self-
sufficient democratic republic. They then go on to
blame the Islamic invaders for disrupting the paradise,
and speak of its recovery when Hindus unite to work
their way through differences of religion, caste, ethnic-
ity, and language to build a strong, self-assertive
nation.

This version of *Hindutva* doesn't seem an advance
over what was proposed by the Hindu reformers of the
nineteenth century: it is a dated solution, a mishmash
of ancient Vedic wisdom, overblown ideas of India's
past glory, and now-forgotten nineteenth-century theories of European nationalism. It offers few practical
ideas about how India can be regenerated; and,
although it seeks to offset the damage done to India by
centuries of a Muslim and British presence, very often,
in its simultaneous and contradictory longing for an
uncomplicated golden age and sophisticated nuclear
technology, it seems merely another consequence of
that damage.

4

- - - - -

MOST OF THE parties that managed to unseat
the Congress in 1977, 1989, and then in 1996, and are

now slowly falling apart, were offshoots or disgruntled splinter groups of the Congress. Their members for the last fifty years have tended to be from the same ruling class as the Congress's leaders; and in recent years they have regularly voted with the Congress against the BJP. The pretext is usually the defense of secularism. Behind it may also lie the not unjustified fear that the BJP may be the first alternative to the Congress to appear in India.

There is an ominous perception of the BJP that the Congress and its offshoots have encouraged, and that has been accepted in the rest of the world. This perception is now likely to be strengthened by the nuclear tests: the perception of the BJP as a sinister political force, almost fascistic, with its disciplined cadres and its complex internal hierarchy, part of the lunatic fringe of Indian politics. Unfortunately, labels like fascist, borrowed from another continent and another kind of politics, do little to explain an Indian phenomenon, rooted in the peculiar exigencies of the country. The BJP can be called an extremist party in the sense that it more forcefully articulates cultural and political aspirations that are already held in more normal, less oppressive forms in Indian society. For instance, the BJP's nuclear tests are no aberration; they enhance an image independent India has tried to have of itself. One reason behind the Indian middle-class euphoria over the tests—which may have struck many people, especially outside India, as unpleasant and anachronistic—is that they represent a step forward in the aim first set out by the Congress, which was to beat the

West at its own game by turning a poor, primarily agricultural country into a heavily industrialized, militarily self-assertive one.

The component of the BJP believed to be the most sinister is the RSS (loosely translated as National Volunteers Organization), which is the parent body of the BJP. Set up in 1925 in order ostensibly to encourage character-building among Hindus (as a first step toward recovering a once-glorious Hindu nation), it has since considerably expanded its membership (the actual number is not known, and there are now branches in the US and UK) and range of activities. Related groups now run a large network of primary schools across India. They organize *Hindutva*-inspired welfare schemes for the tribes living in the forests of Bihar, Assam, Tripura, Arunachal Pradesh, and Madhya Pradesh to compete with the abundant Christian missionaries stationed there; they sponsor earthquake, famine, and flood relief; they run trade unions (the largest trade union in India, the BMS, is controlled by members of the RSS).

The RSS is believed to have a strong influence on the BJP, as might be expected since most of the BJP's leaders were, or are, members. RSS volunteers, who assemble in their uniform of khaki shorts, black caps, and white shirts, belong to a range of professions: members of the armed forces, shopkeepers, teachers, clerks, engineers, doctors, scientists, lawyers, and journalists; they give money (the RSS is self-financed) and time for the organization, which also has its own full-time workers. The RSS holds morning assemblies, where younger volunteers do physical exercises and listen to lectures or talks on Indian history or current events that stress the greatness of Hindu values and the importance of Hindu unity—all part of becoming what a senior leader calls "the shining symbol of Hindu manhood embodying in himself all our traditional values of love, self-restraint, sacrifice, service, and character."

Much of this has a distinct *Ubermensch* ring; and it is right to be suspicious of it, or to see it as the enactment of a middle-class dream of hypermasculinity. But the lower middle classes in small towns from whom the RSS derives its strength respond to it as answering needs that are more and more urgent in the chaos of modern India, where old bonds of family and tradition are giving way to an aggressive consumer culture that touches everyone but can be indulged in by only the affluent few. In India's degraded urban environments, people live perpetually on the edge; rage and frustration are always on the surface; and material deprivation makes things like cultural identity, a sense of community and self, even more valuable. Few organizations in India offer a cultural mooring in quite the same way as the RSS does; and the general failure of the Communist movement in India has meant that educated lower-middle-class youth, lost as they are in the midst of relentless change, are likely to express their disaffection through groups like the RSS.

There is a strong anti-Islamic strain in the RSS's ideology, although it is hard to see how, given the RSS's intention of restoring Hindu pride that has been battered by centuries of Muslim rule, something of the sort could not be there.[5] However, Indian Muslims are an impoverished, politically adrift, and fearful minority, and it is Pakistan that has recently become a favorite target of anti-Islamic feeling. The RSS represents and exploits an awkward Indian reality: a widespread, and almost visceral, distrust and resentment of Islam and Muslims has long existed among large sections of even the educated Hindu population. The destructiveness and intolerance of some of India's Islamic conquerors and rulers may be things of the past; but the politics of religion, of divide and rule, which the British introduced in India for their own benefit—and which eventually led to the bloody vivisection of India—has left a legacy of bitterness among Hindus and Muslims in many parts of India. The Congress profited far more than the RSS or BJP by exploiting this mutual distrust: many of the approximately 8,000 riots between Hindus and Muslims since 1947 are thought to have been engineered by Congress politicians in order to polarize votes along religious lines in particular constituencies.

In fact, the RSS and the BJP are closer ideologically to an exclusivist kind of Hindu assertiveness that was initially part of the Congress but was sidelined once Mahatma Gandhi took over the leadership. Gandhi

---

5. Interestingly, a grudging admiration for the British exists in RSS–BJP circles. Much like Karl Marx, Hindu ideologues in the nineteenth century often spoke of British rule in India as an "unconscious tool of history"—something that would help Hindus pick up the greatest virtues of European civilization on their own way to national greatness.

toned down the exclusionary neo-Hindu image the freedom struggle had projected in the early years of this century, even if he could not cleanse Congress of men who were aggressively, if covertly, pro-Hindu and anti-Muslim in their political outlook; and he did so by personally improvising a kind of soft folk version of Hinduism that he hoped would not alienate Muslims, who were crucial to the success of the freedom movement. The exclusionist strain in Hindu nationalism became more marginal as Gandhi's methods of nonviolent resistance gradually moved to center stage. In the 1940s the aggressive demand for a separate Muslim homeland, and the Congress's subsequent failure to prevent the partition of India, aroused in many Hindus second thoughts about the direction the freedom struggle had taken under Gandhi and Nehru.

Several small Hindu nationalist groups used this disaffection to revitalize themselves. But they remained dingy backroom affairs, on the fringe, popular only among a few Hindu refugees from Pakistan and a few reactionary Brahmin intellectuals in central and north India. It was one of these groups that was involved in the conspiracy to murder Mahatma Gandhi—a complicated event in that the assassin, like many Hindu nationalists, acknowledged Gandhi's personal greatness, but saw his death as essential to the safety and welfare of Hindu India.

The killing of Gandhi in 1948 made these groups seem even more remote from the rest of the country. Responding to a national mood of revulsion, Nehru banned all the more prominent extremist Hindu groups, including the RSS. There was no evidence that the RSS had anything to do with the assassination, and the ban was soon lifted. Nehru's position softened enough to allow him in 1962 to invite the RSS to participate in the Republic Day parade in New Delhi.

The BJP itself was formed under the name of Jana Sangh, in 1951, ostensibly to carry on in politics the task of nation-building undertaken in social and cultural life by the RSS. For many decades, the party was, like every other opposition party, under the gigantic shadow of the Congress. It was briefly in office with other opposition parties in 1977 and 1989, but coming to power on its own was a distant dream—at least so it must have seemed in the 1984 elections, when it won two seats in the parliament.

It was the Ayodhya movement that strengthened the BJP in the late Eighties, but it has come a long way since then. The party is now aware that the pressing issue for the middle classes is the future of economic reforms, and its emphasis in the recent election was on political and economic stability, not on cultural nationalism: the popular slogan of previous elections, *Garv Se kaho Ham Hindu Hain* ("Say with pride that you are a Hindu"), was not much heard this time. Inspired by the success of Tony Blair's New Labour, party leaders talk now of the "New BJP."

They went to some trouble to distance themselves from the party's cousin organization, the VHP (World Hindu Council), the newest and most aggressive of the three organizations (the RSS and the BJP being the other two) that make up what is known as the Sangh

Parivar (the Sangh Family). The VHP's volunteers, mainly drawn from among temple priests and administrators, heads of ashrams and maths (Hindu approximations of the Vatican), represent the most explicitly extremist religious element in the Sangh Family. The nuclear tests have, for now, weakened their pressures, at least, but in the long run the BJP-led government, no matter how secure its majority, cannot afford to antagonize the already very alienated 120 million Muslims in India.

In its pronouncements, the party offers peace, security, and equal opportunity. At virtually every party meeting, ways of attracting Muslims are discussed. The RSS was able to enlist a few Muslim members; the BJP put up several Muslim candidates in the recent elections, one of whom won and is now a minister in the central government. Moreover, since its growing defection from the Congress, the Muslim vote is up for grabs—a perception that recently forced even Mr. Thackeray to repackage himself as a defender of Muslim interests in India. These promises may not be empty ones, for in states ruled by the BJP there have been fewer violent incidents against the Muslims. Still, much of the Muslim vote went to the Congress in 1998, although it increased support for the BJP from 4 to 7 percent.

Similarly, in the state of Uttar Pradesh the BJP has been successful at manipulating caste politics. In what is the largest political constituency in India, it expanded its old electoral base of upper-caste voters by forming temporary alliances with a Dalit (low-caste) party and appointing low-caste men to important positions in the state government: the result in 1998 was a nationwide 12 percent rise in votes from low-caste voters. Rhetorically, too, the BJP has made a few changes in its official line. Its leaders now claim that the party is the truest heir of the old Congress—the Congress of Mahatma Gandhi and not of Nehru, whom the BJP holds responsible, not entirely unfairly, for many of India's failures. In this view, Nehru is seen as an isolated Anglophile intellectual unaware of the needs and aspirations of the vast Hindu India that only Gandhi and a few other Congress leaders recognized. The perception is well-timed since it coincides with the recent unraveling of the most cherished of Nehruvian ideas of secularism, socialism, and nonalignment.

In effect, the demolition of the Babri mosque in 1992 was the culmination of a long process: the consistent failure of the high-minded secular-rational principles Nehru prescribed for the Congress and the Indian state. The process itself is a part of a larger historical trend: the passing away of the ideas of the first generation of postcolonial leaders—Nasser, Kenyatta, Nehru, Sukarno, glamorous international figures in the 1950s, whose grand vision for their newly independent nations was undermined perhaps inevitably by their successors. Nehru's ideals were cast aside by members of his own family. In fact, in the late 1980s Rajiv Gandhi unsuccessfully tried to steal the Ayodhya platform from the BJP, and even usurped the BJP's promise of restoring Ram Rajya (the golden age of Hindu mythology). His successor, Narasimha Rao, a devotee of various Indian holy men (*The Insider* is dedicated to one of them), was himself a silent spectator of the demolition of the Babri mosque. (He is currently writing a monograph on Ayodhya that will set forth his version of the events leading up to the demolition.)

The demolition caused the greatest anguish among the English-speaking Indian intelligentsia—Nehru's most enduring legacy—a state-subsidized genteel-bourgeois world of broadly left-wing bureaucrats and academics. These intellectuals loathe the BJP and its related organizations, seeing them as Indian versions of Mussolini's black-shirted fascists who will plunge India into civil war with the Muslims.

The secularist ideal, well-meaning but always some-what vague, and backed by little more than the personal example offered by the genuinely secular Nehru, had been just enough to maintain, fitfully, an uneasy cease-fire between Hindus and Muslims after the brutalities of Partition. It depended too much on the goodwill of men like Gandhi and Nehru, which though strong enough to enshrine secularism in India's written consti-tution couldn't erase the long history of Hindu–Muslim antagonism. In the hands of Indira and Rajiv Gandhi, the Nehruvian idea became vulnerable to the increas-ingly strong attacks mounted by the BJP, which called it "pseudo-secularism," a habit of appeasing reactionary elements within the Muslim community who the nation-alists felt had already been appeased enough by being granted a separate homeland in the form of Pakistan.

Throughout the last three decades, Hindu national-ists kept saying that the Congress refused to implement a uniform civil code in the country—an issue on which the BJP and the Communists are in broad agreement— only because it feared losing its support among certain mullahs and imams within the Muslim community. Often, the Congress acted in such a way as to confirm the BJP's accusations that it was cynically pandering for Muslim votes in complete disregard of its own secular principles. In 1986, the government, using its majority in parliament, overturned a progressive Supreme Court ruling that made far-reaching changes in Islamic maintenance laws for women, in order to placate the all-male Islamic clergy which the Congress thought had a strong influence over Muslim voters. It turned the BJP into the unlikely champion of the rights of Muslim women. Successive Congress governments granted special political and economic concessions to the Muslim majority state of Kashmir, which many Indians felt only contributed to Kashmir's isolation, and to its violent secessionist movement which began in 1990.

Support for the BJP's recent decision to hold nuclear tests has also been indirectly strengthened by the threatening increase in small but well-organized Islamic fundamentalist groups across India—one of them was responsible for the bombings that killed sixty people in the South Indian city of Coimbatore during the recent elections. Such events in the past have usually been blamed on India's unfriendly Islamic neighbors on its eastern border, the prime suspect being Pakistan. Separatist movements in Punjab and Kashmir may also have strengthened the BJP's resolve to go nuclear—the most radical rejection yet of Nehru's already partially obsolete foreign policy of peaceful nonalignment and denuclearization.

In the late 1980s and early 1990s, the third of Nehru's projects—state socialism—ran aground. Four decades of protectionism had left the Indian economy stagnant. Most of the government-run heavy and light industries were in the red; exports were falling; the foreign exchange reserves had reached an all-time low. It was at a time of crisis when the Congress government, going against its own professed position, began to open up the economy to foreign investment in 1991; it freed many parts of the economy where entrepreneurs were subject to a labyrinthine and corrupt system of permits. The center in Indian politics made its first clear shift away from the left; and the BJP, then gaining support, was well placed to capitalize on this implicit acknowledgement of the Congress's economic failures.

Although in its rhetoric opposed to any foreign economic presence—there will always be plenty of takers for that line in formerly colonial countries—the BJP was quick to see a new constituency in the middle class created by the resulting new wealth in small cities and towns. Not unexpectedly, it did very well in urban middle-class regions in the recent elections. An overwhelming 49 percent of highly educated voters supported it—almost twice as many as voted for the Congress. This new generation of Indians is drawn to the party it sees as the most reliable guarantor of economic reforms—a perception also endorsed by the big corporations, several of which financed the BJP's expensive and slick election campaign.

5

- - - - -

T H E   C H O I C E   O F   a liberal-seeming prime minister and change in rhetoric are all matters of image making. Besides its position on the nuclear issue, what will
be closely examined in the next few months is the B J P's
ability to tackle corruption—the greatest problem for
many Indians. Corruption came to be institutionalized
across India during Mrs. Gandhi's tenure in the Seventies and early Eighties through a selective distribution
of state patronage: public projects had illegal commissions written into them; large underhand paybacks
were received from foreign arms sellers (something that
eventually tripped up her son Rajiv); government officials in important positions and senior politicians, if
they wanted to get anywhere, had to arrange for regular transfusions of money into the Congress's kitty. As
Rao puts it in *The Insider*, "When it came to maintain-
ing a Delhi lobby, some chief ministers had to talk
mainly with money." Even promotions of minor civil
servants required transfers of large sums of money; so
did admissions to schools and colleges.

The rot has traveled all the way down from the
highest office in the land, where Rao himself was
accused of having received a suitcase full of sixty lakh
rupees, or $150,000. You now often need to bribe
people to get an ordinary rail ticket, or to have your
telephone repaired. A news magazine recently featured
a primer of sorts on corruption in India: how much

264

to pay your child's schoolteacher for enhanced grades, how much for a water connection, and that sort of thing. No irony was intended; the figures given were accurate.

Fifty years after Independence, politics is now little more than an investment opportunity, an idea uncynically accepted in public discourse where a politician's career is assessed with respect to the wealth he has amassed. The new "men of the soil," the politicians from Dalit and other so-called backward castes, are only more recent examples of a political culture that was spawned by the Congress, a culture in which being a member of the ruling class is all too often a license for criminal activity. The new politicians' several years of power in some Indian states have created a creamy layer of rich landlords and businessmen; for the millions underneath them, the disused public parks and broken roads renamed after low-caste politicians are the sole benefits from self-rule.

The most influential casteist politician in India is Laloo Prasad Yadav, the former chief minister of the state of Bihar. Yadav draws his strength from his carefully cultivated image as a messiah for members of his Yadav caste and for Muslims, both of whom are numerous in Bihar. His career could serve as an illustration for the theory offered by Chaudhury in *The Insider*: "Political power is the only means by which you can serve the poor in an underdeveloped country like India. So you have to be in power continuously, for the sake of the poor. If you happen to get rich en route that is only incidental. And logically, therefore, whatever you do to gain power is legitimate, since it is meant for the poor."

Yadav was implicated last year in a series of spectacular scams involving the import of cattle fodder: he is charged with pilfering close to $300 million from the state treasury. After warrants for his arrest were issued by the Central Bureau of Investigation in Delhi, he turned his official residence into a fortress; and when it looked as if the army might be called in to deal with his armed defenders, he led a long procession to the local court and surrendered before a cowering judge—but not before he had appointed his wife chief minister. His prison turned out to be a luxurious government guest house from where he continued to issue fiats and decrees. He was released on bail to contest the recent elections, where, amid accusations of seriously corrupt electoral practices (organized, allegedly, by his wife), he and his supporters won seventeen seats in the national parliament.

The BJP promises change, but whether or not it is serious about this it is probably too late to make much difference. In any event, there is increasing evidence that it is not averse to the status quo. It has promoted legislators with criminal records to key ministerial positions in order to prop up its fragile majority in the state legislature of Uttar Pradesh. One of the candidates it has backed for the central parliament was a convicted criminal with twenty-five pending cases against him, including six for murder; he lost to someone who had thirty-five criminal charges against him. Charges have been made against the party's own leaders, although most have so far been known for their personal probity.

The social climate for the BJP-led government is no more propitious than it was for any other governments in the past. The always fragile ideas in India of democracy and egalitarianism have been further enfeebled by the grab-all-you-can mentality spawned by the economic reforms among their prime beneficiaries, the new middle class. The narrow concerns of this class are best reflected by the English-language press and television, which, apart from a handful of exceptions, is even more confused about its role in a semiliterate third world democracy. It is certainly slicker, bigger, and more self-confident than in the days of the Emergency, when, if it was told to bend, as one imprisoned opposition leader, L. K. Advani, a BJP hard-liner who is now home minister, famously put it, it *crawled*.

However, much of the slickness and confidence seems devoted to covering the bogus celebrities and events of the new fashion and entertainment industry— the cultural offshoot of the liberalized economy. Cindy Crawford is coming! Cindy Crawford is coming! crows a serious news magazine, and over the next few days, both on TV and in print, the nation is made to follow closely Crawford's promotional jaunt on behalf of Omega watches. Sixty-four Dalits are massacred in one village in Bihar by private armies hired by upper-caste landlords, and the news barely made it to the front pages, where news of another Indian woman winning the Miss World contest had made headlines. The largest-circulation English-language newspaper, *The*

Times of India, recently started a Human Rights Watch
column after the ailing owner of the Times newspaper
group, Ashok Jain, was prevented from going abroad
for medical treatment by authorities investigating his
financial misdemeanors. After weeks of remaining preoccupied with Mr. Jain's problems, with many damaging stories about his tormentors, the column now seeks
to explain its new-found obsession with human rights.
A recent headline reads: "All newspapers should focus
on human rights violations: Justice P. B. Sawant."

"A nation ceaselessly exchanging banalities with
itself," V. S. Naipaul wrote in 1967, at a low moment
in India's post-Independence history, and the remark
seems even truer now. The breakdown of the legal
system and the assault on civil liberties, the routine
torture of prisoners (in a bizarre incident last month,
senior air force officers asking for a pay raise were
arrested and forced to sit on electric heaters), the custo-
dial deaths and extrajudicial killings—such common
and disturbing symptoms of the deep malaise in the
democratic system are not much noticed by affluent
Indians, and nobody knows what the BJP proposes to
do about them.

Despite its popularity after the nuclear tests, the BJP
has still not freed itself from the contradictory positions of its coalition partners. The defense portfolio,
for instance, is handled by a maverick old socialist who
is a fervent supporter of the Tibetan cause, something
not very high on the BJP's own agenda. In foreign
affairs, the policies of the BJP, having now cashed its
nuclear card, are likely to be directed by its domestic

fortunes. Relations with both Pakistan and China have been set back a few years by the nuclear tests, and may well deteriorate further—particularly with the former. The friendly relations with Russia, which has refused to impose sanctions on India, will remain. And, despite what it says in public, the BJP wants relations with Western countries restored to normal as soon as possible: one powerful reason is its well-to-do Indian supporters in the United States and Britain who have been helping to bankroll the party's political campaigns.

There are also many local factors, such as the state government of Andhra Pradesh, whose support at present gives the government a wafer-thin majority in parliament and whose leaders may be worried about the possible impact of sanctions on the state economy, which depends on foreign investment. Once normal relations are restored, the BJP will probably try to advance the process of seeking closer military cooperation with the United States, in order to create a strong bulwark against China.

But the government's biggest test lies in dealing with the deteriorating condition of hundreds of millions of Indians. It is not a matter about which the BJP has ever been called upon to do much, and the statistics suggest they have got their work cut out for them. 226 million Indians are without safe drinking water; 640 million without basic sanitation; 291 million are illiterate; 44 percent of the population (one third of the world's poor) lives in absolute poverty.

India's poor have borne the brunt of the food price rises that were partly caused by exposing the economy

to the chaotic fluctuations of supply and demand in
international markets. The prices of wheat and sugar
have risen to new levels; the government had to ban the
export of onions, which, along with a piece of bread,
constitute the sole meal of the day for many Indians living below the poverty line, and whose price, after a bad
crop, has gone up three times in the last few months.

The BJP's main constituency, too, is in trouble. Six
years of economic reforms, while making the poor
poorer, increased middle-class consumerism. But the
reforms are faltering; the economy is in deep recession.
The crises of Southeast Asia haven't reached India—
yet. But the flow of foreign investment has dried up.
Property prices in Delhi, Bombay, and Bangalore, once
as high as in Manhattan and Tokyo, have slumped.
Many Indian companies have announced drastic
retrenchment plans. Desperate price cuts have been
announced on foreign consumer brands such as Nike,
Reebok, and Levi's; they have proved too expensive for
Indian consumers. After heavy losses, multinationals
such as Sony and Kellogg are drastically revising their
plans for India. To most of these multinational companies the much-trumpeted 200-million-strong middle
class of India has proved disappointing: Mercedes-
Benz, hoping to sell 10,000 cars a year, sells only forty
and fifty every month. Peugeot's joint venture with an
Indian company is near collapse. The accumulated
losses of top companies like Whirlpool, General
Electric, Sony, Panasonic, Coca-Cola, and Pepsico are
estimated at $375 million.

However, investments by multinational companies

are expected to continue despite disappointing results so far; and they are unlikely to be much affected by the sanctions imposed by the governments of the US, Japan, and Canada after the nuclear tests. Since they stand to lose their own money, multinational companies are only likely to put pressure on the G-8 governments for a more tolerant attitude toward India: Boeing is already nervous about a deal with Air India that it fears may now go to Airbus. After announcing the cancellation of $1 billion in aid to India, the Japanese government soon slashed the figure down to $26 million and then said that all projects already approved would go through. Indeed, most of the EU nations, including Britain and France, are unwilling to impose any sanctions. Clinton's own sanctions, which involve cutting off government aid, canceling credit loans and guarantees, and impeding World Bank and IMF loans to India, are expected to merely pinch, and not hurt, the Indian economy. Some infrastructure projects in the power and telecom sector are likely to be slowed down; the rupee, which has been shaky for some time against the dollar, has slipped, but may end up finding what experts call a realistic and desirable level.

Soon after the the events in Tiananmen Square, the Chinese government put together an irresistible package of reforms for foreign investors; the investments it attracted neutralized the effect of international sanctions and spurred faster GDP growth. A day after the tests, the BJP government announced the opening of the housing sector to foreign investment and then cleared a long-delayed mining license to a US company. There are other indications that the BJP government is following China's example, by pushing at a greater pace the liberal reforms which opened up India to foreign investors seven years ago. In fact, the sanctions are being perceived as an opportunity of sorts by the Indian proponents of economic reforms, whose recent sluggish implementation has led to the current recession. Only last month India's new finance minister was in the US, where he appeared before the editorial board of *The Wall Street Journal* in a bid to reassure American investors, who have the largest stake among all foreign investors in India, about the BJP-led government. (When asked about *Swadeshi*—the BJP's catchall term for economic self-reliance—he dismissed it as a state of mind.)

The sanctions may isolate India within the international community—but only for a time. The example of France is not unfamiliar to the Indian government, which very clearly knew that sanctions would not seriously undermine the Indian economy. France faced a similar sort of international outrage after its nuclear tests[6]; but the dust soon settled after it signed the Comprehensive Test Ban Treaty. It is likely that after establishing India's claims to the nuclear club before the world (and having in the process ensured its own survival, if only temporarily), the BJP government will adopt a conciliatory position. It is already talking of

---

6. India did not join in the international outcry against France, which has now reciprocated in kind and has even opposed US sanctions.

formalizing its self-declared moratorium on nuclear tests and may sign, after some token reservations and objections, the CTBT, which the last Indian government rejected, thus making it easier for the G-8 countries to do business with India again.

A stable government might have inspired more confidence among foreign investors. But for now it looks as if the BJP government can only stay in power by striking dramatic postures, the options for which are at present rather limited. It can't build a temple in Ayodhya, or enact a uniform civil code, without losing its allies and causing riots between Hindus and Muslims across India; it can't cancel the special concessions granted to Kashmir without reviving the secessionist movement that has shown signs of flagging. It can, however, keep pressing the hot buttons of Pakistan and China and raising alarms about national security without any loss in domestic support. Now Pakistan's own nuclear tests have made it easier for the BJP to raise the bogey again. Faced with now-growing criticism for having initiated a nuclear arms race, the BJP is only likely to step up its jingoistic talk.

The jingoism would play a major part in the BJP's preparations for the next round of elections. Large rallies meant to celebrate India's emergence as a nuclear superpower are scheduled to be held in the next few weeks; party leaders are meant to go out and educate the masses about threats to India's unity. If new elections take place by the end of this year, the Hindu Pride card is likely to return the BJP to power with a clearer majority. Until then, many members of the government will make as much money as they can during their brief tryst with state power.

You get a strong feeling of déjà vu—particularly when you consider the disproportionate amount of public time and energy that in India is diverted into futile political speculation. As 600 million Indians went to the polls in February, an army of pundits and psephologists took over TV screens across India; and the air grew thick with their talk of "swings" and "caste" percentages. For days and nights on end, they discussed events and personalities about whom the most accurate thing one could say was that they would soon be overtaken by events and personalities equally inconsequential.

Increasingly, the surface eventfulness of Indian politics turns out to be a deceptive thing; and the scientific jargon employed to explain it seems to be obscuring a very basic fact: that the political system, when assessed, as it should be, on the basis of its own home-grown deformities, has long abnegated its basic responsibilities to the needy millions, India's invisible majority, and survives only through its ability to enrich people venal enough to be part of it. Democracy in India—that much-celebrated accomplishment—seems to have degenerated into a vast colorful circus of almost continuous elections. And now, as the economy stumbles, and tough times, after the current euphoria, loom ahead for the middle class, the poor may find that the small portions of bread that occasionally went with the circuses have become even smaller.

MAY 28, 1998

by Dr. Gowri Ramnarayan,
music critic and journalist

1.

HEMANT CHAUHAN
"Naam bina kachhu na miley"
(excerpt)
3:36

from FOLK MUSIC OF INDIA, courtesy of Music Today, New Delhi, India

This prayerful verse from the folk music of Gujarat is philosophical in content. It states unequivocally that the name of God is the key to eternal bliss and that life is worthless without chanting his name. It also emphasizes the mystical relationship between the disciple and the guru, who guides the seeker toward God. The slow upsurge of melody, with its elongated notes and oscillations, is structured to underscore feelings of adoration and conviction, and demonstrates the high levels of sophistication folk music can achieve when sung by a trained voice.

The song is accompanied by the chautara (a four-stringed instrument), the tabla (the twin drums used in both classical and lighter forms of music in North India), the naar (a drum of the region), and manjira (cymbals, which are an essential part of devotional music all over the country).

2.

CHORUS
"Red pakke royelo"
(excerpt)
2:39

from FOLK MUSIC OF INDIA, courtesy of Music Today, New Delhi, India

This is one of the thirteen forms of *natti*, an exuberant folk song for group dancing prevalent in Hindi-speaking Himachal Pradesh.

Each variant of *natti* has its own tempo, set by the pounding rhythm of two drums called the dholak and the dafli. The latter resembles the tambourine. The rhythms bring their own mounting excitement as well as continuity to the characteristic refrains.

This kind of group singing serves the purposes of ritual, entertainment, and community bonding all over India. Here, in the chorus led by Mohan Rathore, the women repeat the verses sung by the men for emphasis and effect. The drum and bells, as well as the shrill, sharp flute, play a prominent role in adding zest to the proceedings. The language is a dialect from Upper Mahasu, a famous apple-growing region of Himachal Pradesh.

3.
JASVINDER YAMIA
"Dhola"
(excerpt)
2:35

from FOLK MUSIC OF INDIA, courtesy of Music Today, New Delhi, India

The plaintive introduction of strings and drum beats sets the mood for a Punjabi love song in which a man describes his feelings as he pines for his beloved. In literal translation, the opening line exclaims with urgency, "Listen, oh, listen, my heart is flying away!" The lover is always filled with dreams of the young woman who is far away from him. Whenever he plays the drum, he sees the image of her dancing to it.

The rhythm, set to a medium tempo with an irregular arrangement of 3+2+2, suggests accelerating heartbeats, while the fading notes at the end of the verse simulate a long, drawn-out sigh. The purity of the singing voice creates its own magic. The language is a dialect whose musical syllables add poignancy to the sentiment expressed. The mandolin is used here as are the dholak and another drum called the chipdi for percussion.

4.

PANDIT HARIPRASAD CHAURASIA (flute)

276 Raag Bairagi: Alaap & Gat in Ektaal

(excerpt)

3:24

from FLUTE FANTASIA, courtesy of Super Cassettes Industries Limited, Noida, India

Ragas are basic melodies that Indian musicians use as source material for improvisation. They are usually associated with a time of day or season of the year at which they should be performed, and particular sentiments or expressive purposes may also be attributed to them.

Here India's foremost living flautist, Hariprasad Chaurasia, performs an *alaap*, an improved expansion of a raga without rhythm accompaniment, followed by a *gat*, a composition with rhythm accompaniment. Both are in the morning raga called Bairagi, a raga of relatively recent origin created by the famous sitarist Ravi Shankar. It has a meditative quality, brought out by Chaurasia's resonance in the long-held notes.

Chaurasia plays the Indian bamboo flute. The musician holds it sideways, blowing into the first hole and fingering the others directly without the aid of keys, as with the Western instrument. This flute is a very old instrument associated with Lord Krishna, which was used to accompany ancient Vedic chants and Buddhist religious music. In addition to its important role in classical music, it is employed extensively in folk music all over India.

5.

LATA MANGESHKAR

"Sari sari raat"

3:10

from GOLDEN VOICES, courtesy of EMI The Gramophone Company Limited, Calcutta, India

"My memories of you haunt me all night," laments the lovelorn heroine (Geeta Bali) of the 1958 Hindi potboiler *Ajee Bas Shukriya* in the celebrated voice of Lata Mangeshkar, Indian cinema's enduring dubbing singer, who has lent her voice to three generations of leading ladies. With lyrics by Faruq Kaiser and music by Roshan, "Sari sari raat" ("All night") is typical of the film music of the 1950s, with melodies based in raga music but frequently borrowing from other traditions, including European and Latin American. Note the orchestration that accompanies the song, a concept successfully adapted from the West by Indian cinema. In this number, the score complements the dance movements of the heroine to perfection.

6.

BIKRAM GHOSH
"Khandam—A Sequence of Five"
3:46

from TALKING TABLA, courtesy of Music of the World, Chapel Hill, North Carolina

This tabla piece is played by Bikram Ghosh, a well-known percussionist from West Bengal. The tabla consists of a pair of drums placed in front of the drummer, who is seated on the floor. In Hindustani or North Indian classical music, it usually serves as percussion accompaniment to vocal or instrumental music, with the tabla player sitting to the right of the main performer. But here we are listening to a solo recital.

This piece features a *taal*, or rhythm cycle, of five beats (1-2, 1-2-3). We follow the *taal* first through hand claps, then by vocal recitation of the rhythm syllables, and finally on the tabla, in a structured progression of patterns from slow to fast, simple to complex.

7.

RITU GUHA
"Aha tomar sange"
3:04

from GEMS FROM TAGORE, courtesy of EMI The Gramophone Company Limited,
Calcutta, India

Ritu Guha is a well-known exponent of Rabindra Sangeet, a musical genre named after its creator, Rabindranath Tagore, the Nobel

Prize–winning Bengali poet (1861–1941). Tagore set his poems to music, borrowing freely from diverse traditions, both classical and folk, ranging from Hindustani *dhrupad* to Carnatic, or South Indian classical, while giving the musical style he evolved an easily recognizable identity. "Aha tomar sange" ("Oh, with you") is an example of Rabindra Sangeet sung without rhythm accompaniment to underscore a deep philosophical content. Here the human soul yearns for union with the Oversoul, sighing, "Oh, my beloved, my mind is restless without you."

The lyrical value is of prime importance in Rabindra Sangeet, the melodic contours stressing and shading the meanings of the words. The music is preserved and fostered by Viswa Bharati University at Santiniketan in West Bengal, founded by Tagore.

8.

ASHA BHOSLE
"Amar bela je jai"
2:39

from GEMS FROM TAGORE, courtesy of EMI The Gramophone Company Limited, Calcutta, India

Here is another sample of Rabindra Sangeet, performed by Asha Bhosle, veteran dubbing singer of Hindi films and younger sister of Lata Mangeshkar. "Amar bela je jai" ("My day passes") is a light folksy tune with an easy flow and lilt, refracting a joyous exuberance. The song addresses the Lord with confident hope, "I am making constant efforts to mingle my voice with yours." One of the most versatile singers in Indian cinema, with a repertoire ranging from Indian classical to "Indipop," or Indian pop music, the sixty-plus-year-old Asha Bhosle enjoys a keen following among MTV addicts as well as devoted Indian film music audiences.

9.

IQBAL JOGI AND ENSEMBLE
Pahari (Snake Charmers) (excerpts)
2:02
from GREETINGS FROM INDIA, courtesy of Peter's Music Factory, Haarlem, Holland

Pahari in Indian music refers to a basic combination of notes, limited in scale, with regional variations found in the music of the mountains of North India, especially Kashmir. Here the instruments are the algosa, the double flute indigenous to the state of Haryana, as well as the folk form of the been, an ancient stringed instrument. An earthen pot, matka, is used for percussion. This light tune is the kind often heard in country fairs and festivals and is actually played by snake charmers.

10.

GEETA DUTT
"Mera naam chin chin chin"
from the film *Howrah Bridge* (music by O. P. Nayyar)
4:30
courtesy of EMI The Gramophone Company Limited, Calcutta, India

This song from a super-hit crime thriller of 1958 is a dance number in a nightclub scene, made memorable by the vivacious Helen, who brilliantly performs the Hollywood-inspired hybrid music and dance sequences that are still an essential part of the Indian "formula film." The accordion, guitar, saxophone, cello, violin, and drums provide the background to the sultry voice of Geeta Dutt, nee Roy, known more for her slow, sad songs. Although this song was a runaway success, Geeta Dutt was soon to be replaced in the popularity charts by the sisters Lata Mangeshkar and Asha Bhosle.

11.

KADRI GOPALNATH (saxophone)

Tillana — Kadanakutuhalam — Adi

2:47

from SAXOPHONE INDIAN STYLE, courtesy of Bharat Records International Pvt. Ltd.,

Madras, India

Indian classical music has from time to time adapted Western instruments to brilliant effect. These have become permanent fixtures of the Indian concert stage. A recent success story has been that of Kadri Gopalnath, the charismatic saxophone player of Carnatic music. Gopalnath first heard the saxophone in the Mysore Royal Band and made it his own when he modified the instrument to suit the modulations and graces of the Carnatic system. Here he is playing a *tillana*, a rhythm-dominant number of the dance repertoire, in the raga called Kadanakutuhalam. Most ragas are of ancient origin but this one is a nineteenth-century melody inspired by the music of British bands in South India and based on straight notes, as distinct from the curves and glides of Indian classical music. The song is set to *Adi tala*, a rhythm cycle of eight beats (4+2+2). Gopalnath, who has performed with Western musicians in fusion efforts in various countries, is accompanied here by a mridangam, the two-headed drum played by hand, an essential part of Carnatic music.

12.

BAULS OF BENGAL

"Kalkatou mon hashekeley"

4:29

from PURNA DAS BAUL, courtesy of Crammed Discs, Brussels, Belgium

Bauls are wandering minstrels of Bengal who sing devotional songs of deep spiritual content couched in simple language, understood by the person on the street. For example, this song says: "We have come to this world for a short while, to play around for a single lifetime. On the appointed day, we must vacate this place for another destination."

The saffron-clad, long-haired Bauls sing to the accompaniment of the one-string (ektar) or two-string (dotar) lute. Alms are offered to them in the form of food or money as they go from place to place. When Bauls meet they often sing together with great spiritual fervor, aided by ganja, the Indian equivalent of marijuana. Their faith is more philosophical than religious.

13.

U S T A D   B I S M I L L A H   K H A N   (shenai)
Raag Lalit
(excerpt)
4:53

from SHAAN-E-SHENAI, courtesy of Super Cassettes Industries Limited, Noida, India

The shenai is a North Indian wind instrument. This excerpt begins with an *alaap* by the eminent octogenarian shenai player Ustad Bismillah Khan, who resides in the holy Hindu city of Benares, or Varanasi. It is followed by a *gat*, or composition, with rhythm accompaniment. The shenai is considered an indispensable instrument. No festive occasion in North India is complete without it. Here Bismillah Khan expands raga Lalit, a dawn melody of wistful poignancy. The composition is in *teen taal*, a rhythm cycle of sixteen beats, set here to a medium tempo. He is accompanied by a second shenai player and percussion support on the tabla.

14.

S A B R I   B R O T H E R S
"Khwaja ka diwana"
(excerpt)
6:00

courtesy of Xenophile, Danbury, Connecticut

"Khwaja ka diwana" ("I am a devotee of Khwaja Nizamuddin Aulia [a Sufi saint]") is a *qawwali* by the Sabri Brothers of Pakistan, renowned exponents of this form of music, which came to India with Islam. It belongs to the Sufi mystic tradition, which exalts universal love. Music is an important means of reaching God, according to the Sufis, and this is reflected in the spiritual content of *qawwali* music as performed by the Sabri Brothers. Repetition and choral singing are essential elements of *qawwali* music, the singers challenging one another in a mounting frenzy of religious fervor.

15.

A M J A D   A L I   K H A N   (sarod)
Raga Kamalshree
(excerpt)
3:45

from MAESTRO'S CHOICE, courtesy of Music Today, New Delhi, India

The raga Kamalshree played here by Ustad Amjad Ali Khan was created by him as a tribute to the Indian Prime Minister Rajiv Gandhi. The excerpt is from the later part of an exposition in a faster tempo in *teen taal*, played on the sarod to tabla accompaniment.

Amjad Ali Khan belongs to a family whose musical lineage goes back seven generations. He is a member of the Senia gharana, a school of music named after Tansen, a venerated musician of the court of Akbar, the great Moghul. The sarod is a descendant of the Persian rabab, which Amjad Ali Khan's ancestors modified to suit the sophisticated demands of Hindustani classical music. The performer places it on his lap and plays its strings with a plectrum.

16.

D R .   M .   L .   V A S A N T H A K U M A R I
"Vararaga laya"
3:45

from THE LEGEND, courtesy of Sangeetha Koel, Asia One Stop, Poona, India

A pioneering woman vocalist of Carnatic music, M. L. Vasanthakumari (1928–1990) ventured into hitherto male territory in improvised music, challenging the men of the day with her creativity on stage. This piece, a song by Tyagaraja (1767–1847), the revered saint-composer, does not contain any improvisational elements as performed here. "Vararaga laya" is a paean of praise to the power of music in the hands of experts. It also makes sarcastic jibes at those who pretend to be masters of the art.

This is a particularly fast-paced song that typifies Vasanthaku- mari's style and includes decorative solfa syllables for effect. The raga is the rare Chenchukhamboji and the *tala* is *Adi* (4+2+2). Accompaniment is provided by the voice of a disciple, the violin, the mridangam, and the ghatam, a clay pot which is often used as a second percussion instrument in a Carnatic music concert.

17.
PANDIT RAVI SHANKAR
"Mishra Ghara dhun"
(excerpt)
4:17

from MAESTRO'S CHOICE, courtesy of Music Today, New Delhi, India

This beautiful, light romantic, late-evening raga, Mishra Ghara, is played by Pandit Ravi Shankar, arguably the best-known living Indian musician in the world and a recipient of the Bharat Ratna, India's highest civilian honor. He introduced Indian music to Western audiences all over the world with the sitar, a stringed instrument of North India. Here Ravi Shankar plays a raga reserved for the tail end of a concert, after the major melodies. As signified by the term *Mishra* (blend), this tune is embellished by elements extraneous to the raga Ghara. Ravi Shankar lives and teaches Hindustani music mostly in the United States—his disciples at one time included the Beatles—but visits India every year to perform during the winter music season. In this piece, he is accompanied by the tabla.

18.

PANDIT BHIMSEN JOSHI

Raag Malkauns

4:41

from IN CELEBRATION, Volume 2, courtesy of Navras Records Ltd., London, England

The foremost exponent of the Kirana gharana school of Hindustani music founded by the late Abdul Karim Khan, the septuagenarian Pandit Bhimsen Joshi continues to give spirited concerts in his full-blooded voice, with ardent devotion to God and his art. Here he expounds the evening raga called Malkauns in a *khyal* composition set to *teen taal* in a medium tempo. It describes the pangs of a woman neglected by her lover, who favors another.

The romantic lyric has a spiritual dimension to it, the woman and her lover actually depicting the devotee and his God. Joshi is supported by a vocal accompanist, harmonium, and tabla. The harmonium is yet another relic of the British Empire that has come to stay in Indian music, both classical and devotional.

19.

N . RAJAM (violin)

Dadra in Raga Bhairavi

(excerpt)

3:09

from MAESTRO'S CHOICE, courtesy of Music Today, New Delhi, India

The violin was introduced into Carnatic music in the eighteenth century by the musician Baluswami Dikshitar, who first heard it in the army band at Fort St. George, Madras. For Indian music, it is played with the musician seated on the floor, holding it between his or her shoulder and lap. In Hindustani music it is usually a solo instrument, but in the Carnatic system it is also used to accompany vocal and other instrumental music.

N. Rajam was trained rigorously in Carnatic music and, after accompanying senior musicians for years, switched to Hindustani music under the tutelage of the immensely respected vocalist Omkarnath Thakur. She is acclaimed for her sweet and lilting use of the bow and her style of playing, which is closely modeled on vocal techniques. Here she plays a *dadra*, a light sensuous number set to a sprightly rhythm cycle of six beats. Fostered by the courts of North India, *dadra* specializes in descriptions of romantic love in the different seasons, the beauty of the song typically coming from its delicate and nuanced improvisations. This composition is in the raga Bhairavi, which is usually performed at the end of a Hindustani music concert.

285

20.

S M T .   M . S .   S U B B U L A K S H M I
"Rama simira"
3:38

from THE GOLDEN COLLECTION, courtesy of EMI The Gramophone Company Limited, Calcutta, India

This devotional song composed by Guru Nanak of Punjab, the founder of Sikhism, advocates renunciation and surrender to God, since worldly life is but an illusion. It is set in the light Hindustani raga called Pilu. The singer is the great South Indian musician M. S. Subbulakshmi, whose voice has mesmerized three generations of listeners. Recipient of the Bharat Ratna, Subbulakshmi has been a performing artist for over six decades. Steeped in the orthodox Carnatic tradition, she has over the years included songs from other parts of India in her concerts and this has contributed to her appeal throughout India. This excerpt belongs not to her traditional Carnatic repertoire, but draws on other traditions.

Subbulakshmi has sung at the United Nations headquarters, Carnegie Hall, the Edinburgh Festival, and Rachmaninoff Hall in Moscow. At eighty-two, she is a revered figure, adored for her pure voice, her chaste rendering of lyrics, and the spiritual dimension she brings to her music.

Music credits © 1999 The New York Review of Books
© 1999 Art in Concert

ABOUT THE TYPE

The text type, Sabon, was designed by the son of a letter-painter, Jan Tschichold (1902–1974), who was jointly commissioned in 1960 by Monotype, Linotype, and Stempel to create a typeface that would produce consistent results when produced by hand-setting, or with either the Monotype or Linotype machines.

The German book designer and typographer is known for producing a wide range of designs. Tschichold's early work, considered to have revolutionized modern typography, was influenced by the avant-garde Bauhaus and characterized by bold asymmetrical sans serif faces. With his Sabon design, Tschichold demonstrates his later return to more formal and traditional typography. Sabon is based upon the roman Garamond face of Konrad Berner, who married the widow of printer Jacques Sabon. The italic Sabon is modeled after the work of Garamond contemporary, Robert Granjon.

In Sabon, Tschichold's appreciation of classical letters melds with the practicality of consistency and readability into a sophisticated and adaptable typeface.

Sabon is a registered trademark of
Linotype-Hell AG and/or its subsidiaries

Printed and bound by R. R. Donnelley & Sons,
Harrisonburg, Virginia

Interior design by Red Canoe, Deer Lodge, Tennessee
Caroline Kavanagh
Deb Koch